EVANGELICALS AT
THE BRINK OF CRISIS

1966 Gurney Evangelism Lectures, New Orleans Baptist
Theological Seminary, New Orleans, Louisiana

1967 Wieand Lectures, Bethany Theological Seminary,
Oak Brook, Illinois

1967 Lectures, Pensacola Theological Institute,
Pensacola, Florida

EVANGELICALS AT THE BRINK OF CRISIS

Significance of
The World Congress On
Evangelism

BY CARL F. H. HENRY

WORD BOOKS **WACO, TEXAS**

EVANGELICALS AT THE BRINK OF CRISIS

LIBRARY OF CONGRESS CATALOG CARD NUMBER:
67-21104

CONTENTS

CHAPTER ONE

Introduction

Evangelical Christianity has not only received new prominence through the World Congress on Evangelism, but it has also gained new perspective and promise for the near future. But this same turn of events has brought the evangelical movement to a brink of decision over three major concerns that impinge upon its evangelistic task in the world. These concerns are theological, socio-political and ecumenical.

By every rule of ecclesiastical measurement the World Congress was an event of major Christian importance. It is true that *Time* magazine, while devoting its cover to religious affairs, gave the limelight to radical versions of Protestantism rather than to the emergence of an evangelical world vanguard to evangelize the earth in our generation; it emphasized the controversial Bishop James A. Pike above the events in the Berlin Kongresshalle from October 25 to November 4, 1966. But that newsmagazine's religion editor may simply have been reflecting the strategic situation in organized Protestantism, where evangelistic vitality has sagged and theological confusion reigns. Meanwhile in Berlin participants from 100 nations, from 76 church bodies both inside and outside the World Council of Churches, met in a spectacular display of evangelical unity on the basis of biblical theology and evangelism. The delegates' dramatic mile-long march on Reformation Sunday from Wittenbergplatz to Kaiser Wilhelm Memorial Church was the first such public act of witness in Berlin in four centuries, indeed, since a Sunday in December, 1539, when Brandenburg's Prince-Elector publicly embraced the faith of the Protestant Reformation and led a procession from his castle down to the old Cathedral (now St. Margaret's Church in East Berlin) to introduce Luther's Bible and authorize the Reformation teaching. More than 10,000 Berliners joined in the World Congress act of renewal as the clock in the bomb-scarred church tower struck to signal a new hour.

But it was not for Berlin alone, or even for Germany, that the World Congress held out hope of a better day. Its goal was nothing short of the evangelization of the earth in the remaining third of the twentieth century. The Congress was marked by a sense of corporate concern for the most neglected and most urgent task of the Church of Christ, namely, world evangelism. In some respects reminiscent of the Edinburgh World Missionary Conference of 1910, the Congress in other respects—particularly its inclusion of Christian nationals from around the globe, and its sharp rejection of non-biblical theology and evangelism, and its bold enlistment of the laity in the evangelistic mission of the Church—was an event unique in Christian history. Not even the Protestant Reformation, which won its way in the heartland of Europe, offered anything entirely comparable to this.

The delegates' message to Christian believers everywhere, approved by acclamation in the closing hours of the Congress, surveyed every high and holy obligation of the followers of Christ to mankind in and through the Congress theme:

ONE RACE, ONE GOSPEL, ONE TASK

As participants in the World Congress on Evangelism, drawn from 100 nations and gathered in Berlin in the Name of Jesus Christ, we proclaim this day our unswerving determination to carry out the supreme mission of the Church.

On behalf of our fellowmen everywhere, whom we love and for whom our Saviour died, we promise with renewed zeal and faithfulness to bear to them the Good News of God's saving grace to a sinful and lost humanity; and to that end we now rededicate ourselves before the Sovereign King of the universe and the Risen Lord of the Church.

We enter the closing third of the twentieth century with greater confidence than ever in the God of our fathers who reveals Himself in creation, in judgment, and in redemption. In His Holy Name we call upon men and nations everywhere to repent and turn to works of righteousness.

As an evangelical ecumenical gathering of Christian disciples and workers, we cordially invite all believers in Christ to unite in the common task of bringing the Word of Salvation to mankind in spiritual revolt and moral chaos. Our goal is nothing short of the evangelization of the human race in this generation, by every means God has given to the mind and will of men.

ONE RACE

We recognize the failure of many of us in the recent past to speak with sufficient clarity and force upon the Biblical unity of the human race.

All men are one in the humanity created by God Himself. All men are one in their common need of divine redemption, and all are offered salvation in Jesus Christ. All men stand under the same divine condemnation and all must find justification before God in the same way: by faith in Christ, Lord of all and the Saviour of all who put their trust in Him. All who are "in Christ" henceforth can recognize no distinctions based on race or color and no limitations arising out of human pride or prejudice, whether in the fellowship of those who have come to faith in Christ or in the proclamation of the Good News of Jesus Christ to men everywhere.

We reject the notion that men are unequal because of distinction of race or color. In the name of Scripture and of Jesus Christ we condemn racialism wherever it appears. We ask forgiveness for our past sins in refusing to recognize the clear command of God to love our fellowmen with a love that transcends every human barrier and prejudice. We seek by God's grace to eradicate from our lives and from our witness whatever is displeasing to Him in our relations one with another. We extend our hands to each other in love, and those same hands reach out to men everywhere with the prayer that the Prince of Peace may soon unite our sorely divided world.

ONE GOSPEL

We affirm that God first communicated the Gospel of redemption, and not man; we declare the saving will of God and the saving work of God only because we proclaim the saving Word of God. We are persuaded that today, as in the Reformation, God's people are again being called upon to set God's Word above man's word. We rejoice that the truth of the Bible stands unshaken by human speculation, and that it remains the eternal revelation of God's nature and will for mankind. We reject all theology and criticism that refuses to bring itself under the divine authority of Holy Scripture, and all traditionalism which weakens that authority by adding to the Word of God.

The Bible declares that the Gospel which we have received and wherein we stand, and whereby we are saved, is that "Christ died for our sins according to the Scriptures; and that he was buried, and that he rose again the third day according to the Scriptures" (I Corinthians 15:3-4). Evangelism is the proclamation of the Gospel of the crucified and risen Christ, the only Redeemer of men, according to the Scriptures, with the purpose of persuading condemned and lost sinners to put their trust in God by receiving and accepting Christ as Saviour through the power of the Holy Spirit, and to serve Christ as Lord in every calling of life and in the fellowship of His Church, looking toward the day of His coming in glory.

ONE TASK

Our Lord Jesus Christ, possessor of all authority in heaven and earth, has not only called us to Himself; He has sent us out into the world to be His witnesses. In the power of His Spirit He commands us to proclaim to all people the good news of salvation through His atoning death and resurrection; to invite them to discipleship through repentance and faith; to baptize them into the fellowship of His Church; and to teach them all His words.

We confess our weakness and inadequacy as we seek to fulfill the Great Commission; nevertheless we give ourselves afresh to our Lord and His cause. Recognizing that the ministry of reconciliation is given to us all, we seek to enlist every believer for an effective witness to our world. We long to share that which we have heard, have seen with the eyes of faith, and have experienced in our personal lives. We implore the world Church to obey the divine commission to permeate, challenge, and confront the world with the claims of Jesus Christ.

While not all who hear the Gospel will respond to it, our responsibility is to see that every one is given the opportunity to decide for Christ in our time. Trusting our Lord for strength and guidance, we shoulder this responsibility.

Finally, we express to Evangelist Billy Graham our gratitude for his vision of a World Congress on Evangelism. To the magazine *Christianity Today* goes our debt of thanks for bringing it into reality. As we return to our many fields of labor for Christ we promise to pray for each other; and we extend our love and affection to the whole wide world of men in the matchless Name of our Saviour.

While the driving concern of this statement is evangelistic, its theological, social and ecumenical implications are far-reaching, and in each of these areas the evangelical movement is now strategically stationed at the crossroads in relation to nonevangelical forces in contemporary religious life. The following chapters will deal with these critical areas of engagement. The reader should be forewarned that the World Congress on Evangelism gave nobody an official right to speak for it; hence corporate attribution can only be ventured as a sense of meeting judgment in which, as chairman of the Congress, I hope I have not miscarried the mood of the delegates. One fact of contemporary history is crystal clear. Not only is evangelical Christianity "here to stay," to quote Allen Spraggett's emphatic seven-column headline in the *Toronto Daily Star* (November 5, 1966), but Evangelical Christianity is obviously on the move again. It is making plans for winning men to Christ on a global basis. Its challenge speaks to modern man at every level of life, in this intellectual and social existence no less than his religious outlook.

CARL F. H. HENRY
Editor, *Christianity Today*

CHAPTER TWO

_____

Evangelicals and the Theological Crisis

In the contemporary world of Western thought only three formidable movements insist that man can know ultimate reality.

One is communism, which militantly rejects the reality of the supernatural, and expounds the theory of dialectical materalism on the bold premise that matter or nature is ultimate.

Another is Catholicism. It shares the thesis that man's natural reason can know the nature of being, but contrary to communism it declares unequivocally for supernatural reality. Thomas Aquinas has formulated the classic statement of the Roman Catholic position, and to this day Thomism remains the official philosophy of that church. His familiar "five-fold proof" contends that without appeal to special divine revelation, and by empirical considerations alone, man can give a logically conclusive demonstration of the existence of God, of the soul and of immortality.

The third movement is Evangelical Christianity. Like Catholicism it is unabashedly supernaturalistic, in contrast

7

to communism. But it differs from Catholicism by its epistemological emphasis on the self-revealing God and His authoritative scriptural revelation to man as a rational, moral and spiritual agent created for obedient knowledge, worship, and service of his Maker. In brief, evangelical Christianity also insists that man can know ultimate reality, and that the ultimate reality is supernatural. But it rejects the Thomistic thesis that the reality of God is an empirical inference from sense data. In fact, many evangelical theologians view an empirically-based philosophy—vulnerable as it is to naturalistic counter-attack—as an inadequate exposition of Christian theism. The constant decline of Western philosophy, first from the Biblical theism of the Middle Ages to the speculative theism and idealism of modern philosophy, and then to the naturalism of the nineteenth century, they consider to be a gradual erosion of metaphysical faith that Thomism was powerless to arrest and for which it unwittingly paved the way.

Today the evangelical option not only is an alternative to Roman Catholic theology, it also supplies an alternative to Protestant modernism. In the aftermath of the critical philosophy of Immanuel Kant, who contended that man lacks rational competence to know the supernatural, neo-Protestant theology has increasingly taken an anti-intellectual course; the role of cognitive reason in religious experience has been demeaned; the truth of revelation has been given a subjectivistic cast and deprived of universal validity.

Two transition attempts by neo-Protestant philosophers to vindicate metaphysical idealism on a speculative rationalistic base failed to preserve an intellectual foundation for Protestant modernism. Hegelian idealism collapsed after less than a century of influence, and personalism (represented by the tradition of Lotze-Bowne-Brightman) has steadily diminished in influence. For a small circle of liberal Protestants the philosophy of Alfred North Whitehead or the theology of Paul Tillich provided a temporary detour around extreme anti-intellectual theories, but since these thinkers also rejected the possibility of cognitive knowledge of God, they too reflect a basic concession to the modern religious approach.

As the tide of neo-Protestant theology has swept over the waning currents of philosophical rationalism, a widening sea of anti-intellectualism inundated recent modern religious theory. Influential modernist theologies scuttled the historic Christian view that God reveals Himself intelligibly in valid propositions; no scope remained for receipt of divinely revealed information either in the religious view of Schleiermacher, who located the essence of religion in the feeling of dependence, or in that of Ritschl, who found the center of Christian commitment in trust and excluded assent to supernaturally-given truths. Even Karl Barth made no serious effort in his earliest writings to transcend metaphysical irrationalism; despite his striking emphasis on special divine initiative and disclosure, he held that God cannot be conceptually known; he even insisted, moreover, that only pagan philosophy—and not Christian revelation—espouses cognitive knowledge of God.

As existentialists like Rudolf Bultmann exploited the dialectical theory of religious knowledge, Barth struggled to strengthen the notion of paradox—that every thesis about God requires a complementary antithesis—by affirming that the believer's concepts about God become "adequate" to the knowledge of God through a subjective miracle of grace. But the door remained open to existentialism, with its contention that reality cannot be grasped as a rational system, through Barth's refusal to insist that the truth of relevation is given in the form of propositions universally valid for all men. Similarly Emil Brunner, despite revision of his volume on truth as encounter, declined to the very end to subscribe to the Biblical view that God's self-revelation is intelligibly given in the form of informational statements about His nature and ways.

This surrender of ontological knowledge about God, with its consequent evaporation of valid metaphysical truth, underlies the existentialism of Bultmann. It also shadows the extreme secular views of Mainz radicals like Herbert Braun and Manfred Mezger; of American death-of-God deviationists like Thomas Altizer and William Hamilton; and of linguistic theologians who assign religious terminology a functional rather than ontological significance.

This long train of modern theology has shared one decisive controlling premise, viz., that man does not and cannot have cognitive knowledge of God.

This premise Evangelical Christianity repudiates as inexcusably destructive of genuine metaphysical faith and as antithetical to the scriptural view of revelation.

The World Congress on Evangelism was convened, as its title stipulated, for an evangelistic and soteriological purpose, and not for epistemological and philosophical considerations. But just as the Protestant Reformation had an epistemological no less than a soteriological basis, so the World Congress, too, acted implicitly in the context of a distinctive theory of religious knowledge. No doubt that view—in a setting primarily concerned with evangelism —emerged more often in criticism of alien positions than in the systematic and schematic exposition of evangelical theology. But in the opening remarks of the Congress, in many of the position papers, and in many panel papers, the outlines of a distinctive theology were undeniably present. It was clear that evangelical theology is metaphysically affirmative, in sharp contrast to neo-Protestant religious theory; it is unabashedly supernaturalistic, in direct contradiction to communist materialism; it is confidently revelational and rational, in noteworthy divergence from Thomistic empiricism; it is unapologetically Scriptural, in marked dissent from the Roman Catholic emphasis on tradition and on an authoritative hierarchy.

D. Elton Trueblood has said recently that a remarkable theological opportunity is now open to a rational evangelical Christianity to elaborate a comprehensive world-life view on the basis of divine revelation. The modernist erosion of metaphysical faith has left neo-Protestantism little alternative but to deplore the very ideal of a world view as rationalistic. The haunting collapse of its own earlier speculative reconstructions of metaphysical reality, when coupled with this hardening bent toward anti-intellectual religious theory, will serve to discourage an earnest probing of the evangelical inheritance rooted in Biblical revelation. But the World Congress held resolutely to the historic confidence in God's intelligible self-disclosure and in an authoritative Scriptural revelation. And a noteworthy feature of the Congress was its deepening liaison between evangelical evangelists and theologians. After a generation in which theologians and evangelists have pursued rather independent roles in evangelical circles, Berlin was marked by a frequent plea for the emergence of theologian-evangelists and of evangelist-theologians. In several presentations the anti-intellectual trend of recent theology was recognized as no less a threat to the effective survival of Christianity than was the anti-evangelistic temper of recent ecumenism.

"The mark of our century," says Francis A. Schaeffer of L'Abri Fellowship in Switzerland, "is the victory of the Hegelian concept of synthesis, instead of a recognition of truth in the sense of antithesis and absolutes. . . .Since the influence of Hegel's dialectic and Kierkegaard's 'leap' . . .we are increasingly surrounded by a culture in which the concept of truth in the sense of antithesis, and of moral right and wrong, does not exist. . . .By contrast historic Christianity rests upon truth—not truth as an abstract concept, nor even what the twentieth century man regards as

'religious truth,' but objective truth. . . .To weaken the
historic Christian concept of antithesis is eventually to make
meaningless the personal antithesis of the new birth. If
a clear and unmistakable emphasis of truth, in the sense
of antithesis, is removed, two things occur: first, Christianity in the next generation as true Christianity is weakened;
and second, we will be communicating—in any real sense of
communication—with only that diminishing portion of the
community that still thinks in terms of the older concept
of truth. . . .The unity of orthodox or evangelical evangelism should be centered around an emphasis on *truth* and
not on evangelism as such."

The standing ovation by Berlin delegates to Professor
Johannes Schneider for his stirring advocacy of Biblical
theology and evangelism, as against existential distortions,
signalled an open awareness of the contemporary theological
crisis. Authentic theological communication, stressed
Schneider, requires an avoidance of "the modern mode of
existential philosophy and theology whose anthropological
purpose limits or obscures the Gospel. . . .If the evangelical
sermon is essentially Christocentric then it will be properly
related to all of Holy Scripture. From this center it will
encompass the entire wealth of divine revelation and the
fulness of redemption. . . .To deny the reality of redemption facts is to pull the very foundation out from Christian
faith. . . .The redemptive historical events of Jesus' resurrection is closely related to the salvation fact of Christ's
death. . . .Christ . . .,says Bultmann, was resurrected into
Kerygma. That is, Christ does not continue to live as a
person in a changed form, but as ever-present in the
proclaimed Word. But how can He be active in proclamation if He does not actually exist, inasmuch as His death
ended everything? . . .An evangelism that falls for this
sort of talk is totally without authority. . . .The preacher
or evangelist . . .has no right to interpret the soteriological

statements of the New Testament in merely anthropological or existential terms. . . .It is impossible to speak of the 'significance' of the salvation facts, that is, of the meaning they have for us, if they themselves are disregarded or even denied. . . .When the *Kerygma* is stripped of its revelational historical foundation it simply dangles in thin air. . . . Existential theology likewise knows a concept of decision. . . .There is no word, however, of Christ's atonement as the redemptive-historical foundation of God's forgiving activity."

The existential and subjectivistic outcome of neo-Protestant theology is strong evidence that Barth's principle, namely, the self-revealing God, was too thin a premise to re-establish Biblical Christianity convincingly in the modern religious conflict. Christianity assuredly affirms that God is self-revealed, and indeed—as Barth also insists—that He is self-revealed in Jesus Christ. But it has not historically been infected by a dialectical-paradoxical exposition of divine revelation and redemption. Harold John Ockenga, minister of Park Street Church, Boston, affirms that "the removal of the Bible from the central place of authority in Protestantism has debilitated its power to evangelize." Not only so, but the downgrading of the Bible prepared the way, as Canon Leslie Hunt, principal of Wycliffe College, Toronto, notes, for "the new theology which repudiates the objective view of God and the Biblical concept of sin; and its close associate, the new morality which dismisses the moral law as an outmoded system of moral legalism." No one can doubt that neo-orthodox theology deliberately opposed the authority of divine confrontation to the authority of scriptural revelation. Despite Brunner's acknowledgment that the fate of the Bible is in the long run the fate of Christianity, Barth contended at a colloquium at the University of Chicago that "the Bible is full of errors," and Brunner, in *Revelation and Reason,* saluted critical theories about the Bible as if the Bible were patently false. Yet the conjunction of the truth that *God speaks* with the speculation that the Bible is untrustworthy has now fallen apart through inner contradiction; Christian theology, following the example of Jesus, and of the apostles, must either keep together faith in the self-revealing God and in the scripturally-revealed God, or must surrender both. Hermann Sasse, professor of theology in Immanuel Theological Seminary, North Adelaide, Australia, rightly emphasizes as one of the lessons of history that "we cannot preserve a living faith in the Saviour unless we preserve the doctrine of the Bible concerning His person and work." The emphasis is, in fact, worthy of expansion; the lesson to be learned from contemporary theology is that, apart from reliance on the propositional revelation of the Bible, our knowledge of the self-revealing God is soon overcast by instability and subjectivism. Canon Herbert H. Arrowsmith, general secretary in Australia of the British and Foreign Bible Society, therefore properly stresses the need for calling the corporate Church and individual Christians back to the authority and integrity of Scripture.

The World Congress on Evangelism repeatedly affirmed the integrity and authority of the Bible and repudiated the attacks made upon miraculous supernaturalism by modern scientism. Hans Rohrbach, president of Mainz University, Germany, noted that such criticism usually presupposes the now outmoded nineteenth century philosophy of science. He emphasized, moreover, that the contemporary change in scientific thought gives secular theologians no scientific basis for insisting that there is only one reality, namely, the visible world, so that there cannot be a personal God who acts in both history and nature. "Besides being taught of the existence of the invisible," Rohrbach says, "modern man must be led to experience the reality of the invisible." Samuel J. Mikolaski of New Orleans Baptist Theological

Seminary stressed also that modern man's massive attempts "to show what he can accomplish without any belief in God at all" are not at all due to science, but in part to "scientism" and its skeptical outlook on ethical and religious values.

But the current attacks on the spiritual nature of man derive at their deepest level from the fallenness of man. And many evangelicals now see evidence of man's fallen condition not only in the state of the world but also in the predicament of the visible church. Mikolaski finds this fallenness "exhibited with astonishing clarity" where many ecumenists do not suspect it to exist, that is, in institutionalized religion. "The organized Church increasingly intrudes into public affairs as a social savior while it retreats from the need of godliness in its own life and from the need of getting the Gospel to the common man." A. Morgan Derham, general secretary of the British Evangelical Alliance, notes that the new morality mislocates the primary cause of modern man's resistance to the Gospel in a distaste for legalism and external authority, whereas the primary factor is "the twist in the core of man's being, the corruption we call sin." Concerning man's fallenness, Rohrbach says that "the condition of modern man as fallen man would be hopeless if God had not promised to change man's heart. . . . This therefore is the task and meaning of evangelism: to send co-workers for God with the unabridged message of the cross and resurrection under the sure expectation that God by His Holy Spirit will use their proclamation to accomplish the marvel of quickening man's spiritually dead heart."

What therefore the Church now desperately needs is to recover the truth of revelation and the authoritative note whereby the Protestant Reformation recalled Western Christianity from the welter of tradition and speculation to the teaching of the Bible. Timely indeed is a comment of

Walter Künneth, professor of systematic theology in Erlangen University, "that the much-vaunted effort of modernistic theology to make possible and to simplify Christian faith for today's man is purchased by changing the essential nature of the Gospel. . . . A Gospel that has become cheap is a defeated, emasculated Gospel that can no longer sound a clear trumpet call."

It is well, therefore, to note how the World Congress related its affirmation of an authoritative Bible to the proclamation of the Gospel. Significantly, the statement on Scripture does not stand merely as a preliminary feature of the Congress declaration; it appears under the section on "One Gospel," where it prepares the way for the definition of evangelism. To gauge the importance of this conjunction one must be aware of the prevalent tendency in contemporary ecumenical theology to demean the Bible while supposedly exalting the Gospel, as if these spiritual concerns were quite independent of each other. The juxtaposition of these motifs in the Berlin affirmation reflects the evangelical conviction that in the final outcome the fate of the Gospel and revealed religion cannot now be segregated from the inspiration and reliability of the Bible.

The Congress statement on "The Gospel" therefore begins: "We affirm that God first communicated the Gospel of redemption, and not man; we declare the saving will of God and the saving work of God only because we declare the saving Word of God. We are persuaded that today, as in the Reformation, God's people are again being called upon to set God's Word above man's word."

The World Congress ranged itself not only against speculative criticism of the Bible; it also rejected the dilution of Scriptural authority through appeals to tradition: "We rejoice that the truth of the Bible stands unshaken by human speculation, and that it remains the eternal revelation of God's nature and will for mankind. We reject all theology and criticism that refuses to bring itself under the divine authority of Holy Scripture, and all traditionalism which weakens that authority by adding to the Word of God."

This statement has noteworthy implications for dialogue with the World Council of Churches, but its significance does not stop there. It extends to current proposals that the American Bible Society issue the Bible in an edition that includes the Apocrypha, so that the Roman Catholic Church, which now favors Bible reading by its communicants, need not establish an independent and rival agency. While this issue was not formally discussed in Berlin, delegates would almost indubitably have opposed including the Apocrypha for the sake of ecumenical cooperation, in view of the evangelical distinction between inspired Scripture and fallible tradition. The conciliar readiness to include the Apocrypha is traceable to the neo-Protestant assimilation of the Bible to fallible tradition.

This debate over the unique authority of the Bible involves not merely a matter of literary preference; it raises questions vis-a-vis Evangelical Christianity and Roman Catholicism that were posed by the Protestant Reformation and with which the Vatican Council has not in fact fully come to terms. One of the Roman Catholic observers attending the World Congress on Evangelism was Father John Sheerin, editor of *The Catholic World*. He reported that World Congress criticism of Roman Catholicism was characteristically "theological and made in a good spirit and in all fairness to the Catholic position." But he singled out as a matter of regret "one sentence in the final statement rejecting all traditionalism which adds to the Word of God." Dr. Sheerin added: "The anti-Catholic indictment here has been rendered obsolete by the Council document on Divine Revelation."

But a careful examination of the message of Vatican II shows that while the Roman Church now affirms the inerrancy of Scripture in its soteriological teaching, it nonetheless refuses to distinguish Scripture from tradition, and evangelical criticism at this point is as timely as ever.

On the transmission of divine revelation, the Vatican II document states [excerpts are taken from the English translation in *The Documents of Vatican II,* Walter M. Abbott, general editor (New York: Guild Press, 1966), pp. 116-119] that the "tradition which comes from the apostles develops in the Church with the help of the Holy Spirit. . . . A growth in the understanding of the realities and the words which have been handed down . . . happens through the contemplation and study made by believers . . . and through the preaching of *those who have received through episcopal succession the sure gift of truth* [ital. sup.]. . . . Hence there exists a close connection and communication between sacred tradition and sacred Scripture. . . . It is not from sacred Scripture alone that the Church draws her certainty about everything which has been revealed*. . . .

*Catholic authorities have noted that this foregoing statement was made at the Pope's request in one of the last additions to the text of the document. "It does not exclude the opinion that all revelation is in some way, though perhaps obscurely, contained in Scripture. But this may not suffice for certitude, and in fact the Church always understands and interprets Scripture in the light of her continuous tradition" *(The Documents of Vatican II,* p. 117, n. 21). In evangelical Protestant theology psychological assurance and certainty are derived from the Holy Spirit, not from an authoritative hierarchy.

Both sacred tradition and sacred Scripture are to be accepted and venerated with the same sense of devotion and reverence. . . . Sacred tradition and sacred Scripture form one sacred deposit of the word of God, which is committed to the Church. . . . The task of authentically interpreting the word of God, whether written or handed on, has been entrusted exclusively to the living teaching office**of the

** The *magisterium,* or teaching office, refers in Latin theology to the Pope and the bishops collectively.

Church, whose authority is exercised in the name of Jesus Christ. . . . Sacred tradition, sacred Scripture, and the teaching authority of the Church . . . are so linked and joined together that one cannot stand without the others, and that all together and each in its own way under the action of the one Holy Spirit contribute effectively to the salvation of souls."

While the Vatican II documents affirm that the Scripture teaches "firmly, faithfully, and without error that truth which God wanted to put into the sacred writings for the sake of our salvation," they also affirm that the Roman Church "has always regarded the Scriptures together with sacred tradition as the supreme rule of faith, and will ever do so."

We may see the far-reaching theoretical implications of this debate over tradition through the issues raised in a public discussion in Berlin by Lutheran theologian Walter Künneth and Catholic theologian Karl Rahner during the World Congress, though independently of it. Here the consideration of Scripture and tradition led to the discussion of Mariolatry and of the Church's teaching office. Künneth stressed that the Reformation found its original impulse not in a protest against outward abuses such as indulgences (which Rome from time to time may be quite disposed to reform) but rather in a consideration of the Word of God in Holy Scripture as the only foundation of Christian faith. Does the Catholic Church rank a second source of faith (viz., tradition) alongside the Bible, asked Künneth. Rahner disowned this contrast as a "questionable formulation." Although the Church came about through the living proclamation of the Apostles, he replied, this proclamation was itself reduced to tradition; the Church's tradition is an unfolding of the witness of Scripture. Künneth then inquired whether Scripture is the ground of the Church, or only its product? Rahner thereupon replied that the Church was founded through the apostolic testimony, which finds its written reduction in Scripture; limits cannot be definitely defined, however, so that the question is how to prevent the oral tradition from incorporating into the realm of faith the legends that range themselves alongside the declarations of Scripture.

Künneth then turned to the doctrine of Mariolatry: does not the ascription of special honor to Mary detract from Jesus Christ as the sole mediator between God and man? Here Rahner admitted that a difference exists in the Roman Catholic Church between theory (Christ alone is mediator and redeemer, and Mary is under Him) and practice (as in the Madonna cult reflected not only by the illiterate but even in the prayers of many bishops). But, Rahner added, dogmatic theology ought not to be fashioned out of Sunday-preaching (not even, apparently, from the prayers of bishops?). Künneth replied that there is no basis in Scripture for the immaculate conception and physical assumption of Mary (despite reaffirmation by Pope XII in 1950); hence the pope affirms the physical assumption of Mary on the basis of supposed infallibility. Moreover, the very institution of the papacy stands against Scripture. How can the Church know that its decisions are those of the Holy Spirit? Did not the Roman Catholic Church excommunicate Luther? And what does this imply for an infallible pope?

One of the reporters covering the World Congress, Harold Schachern, who is religion editor of *The Detroit News* and an outstanding Roman Catholic layman, has written that Vatican II seems to offer hope for a convergence that transcends both Catholicism and Protestantism. In an article titled "What Vatican II Means" (December 28, 1966), Schachern emphasizes that theologians of eight major

American denominations endeavoring through the Protestant Consultation on Church Union to shape a 24 million member American Protestant Church "have said without equivocation . . . that they no longer can lean solely on Scripture as the source of divine truth, but must take greater cognizance of the great store of Christian tradition." On the one side, therefore, convergence is furthered by the neo-Protestant assimilation of the Bible to tradition, encouraged not only by the unequivocal Roman Catholic espousal of the full authority of the Old Testament Apocrypha (as clearly shown by the list of canonical books at the Council of Trent, Session IV) but also by the critical views of the Bible advanced by many Roman Catholic scholars today despite their Church's assertion of the inspiration of the Scriptures. But, if Protestants are to surrender Reformation convictions on the unique authority of Scripture and on the canon, what concession to convergence will Rome make on the doctrine of papal infallibility? On this point Schachern's comment is remarkable: "The doctrine of papal infallibility, while appearing at first glance to be a barrier to union of mountainous proportions, actually shrinks in significance when one considers that in the nearly 100 years of existence it has been exercised only once—by Pope Pius XII when in 1946 he defined the doctrine of the assumption of the Blessed Virgin Mary into heaven. It is highly unlikely that this will ever happen again. . . ."

The Catholic advocacy of tradition has important practical implications, not least of all in respect to a new common version of the Bible. One of the welcome changes in the Roman Catholic Church is its new attitude toward the Bible, whose possession and reading by the laity it now welcomes. In fact, cooperative distribution of the Scriptures by Protestants and Catholics is now being encouraged. The Vatican Council decree on divine revelation stated that "easy access to sacred Scripture should be provided for all the Christian faithful" and foresaw cooperation with all "separated brethren," Protestant and Orthodox, in achieving agreed texts. A clear need exists for translations in the common speech of the age, and Roman Catholic scholars are now qualified for a linguistic, textual and exegetical contribution.

At the same time, Roman Catholics have indicated to the American Bible Society that they will not need to form an agency of their own if the Society will issue a version of the Bible that includes the Apocryphal books. Much more is at stake in this bid for ecclesiastical cooperation than the fact that Catholics appeal to the Apocrypha to support such doctrinal aberrations as purgatory. The Reformation churches explicitly denied any status as Scripture to the Old Testament Apocryphal books, whose canonical status the Council of Trent affirms. While their value as ecclesiastical writings was unquestioned, they were rejected as a source of any article of faith.

Surely there must be areas of Bible translation, interpretation and distribution in which Catholics and Protestants can work together. But if the price of ecumenical concord is a Protestant welcome of the Apocrypha alongside the inspired Scriptures, then Protestants can pay such a price only by the surrender of theological integrity.

A new rendering of the Apocrypha is not to be ruled out nor is its inclusion as a separate section, clearly marked as such; if Roman Catholics insist upon interspersing these books among the inspired writings, the only alternative for evangelicals would be to insist on separate Roman Catholic and Protestant editions. But even a Bible that segregates the Apocryphal from the canonical books must be protected against the mistranslation or obscure translation of theological terms. As recently as a century ago, in 1864, Roman Catholic spokesmen condemned the improvement of terms like "do penance" and "charity" to "repent" and "love." Contemporary Catholicism finds repentance and love have become less objectionable, but in Australia, where a joint Bible has been promoted, the Catholic version substitutes the "relatives" of Jesus for His "brethren" to support a dogmatic position. Nor ought Protestants to allow anything in the way of papal imprimatur to intrude upon the final result of a combined effort.

There is no doubt that the Bible itself contains an authentic tradition (as when Paul writes in I Corinthians 15:1-4 of what had been handed down). But the transference of inspired truth is something quite different from the transference of ecclesiastical opinion.

Whether to include the Apocrypha would not today even be a live theological issue in Protestant circles were it not for the modernist attack on the Bible. If the Bible is a fallible book, then the distinction between Scripture and tradition is greatly lessened. From a "fallible" Bible modernism goes to an uncertain theology; from an "obscure" Bible Romanism moves to the Church's infallible teaching office. Harold John Ockenga is wholly right in his contention: "A liberal Protestantism cannot meet the competition of the Roman Church." In the post-Reformation period Rome emphasized the fallibility of the Bible to advance the teaching office of the Church; today Rome emphasizes even the inspiration of Apocryphal books and the certitude of the Church while neo-Protestants doubt the unique inspiration of Scripture and the universal validity of the truth of revelation. The World Congress statement, however, proceeds on a premise other than the fallibility of the Bible and its inherent character as tradition; it presupposes, rather, the inspiration and infallibility of Scripture, its uniqueness in contrast with ecclesiastical tradition, and the answerability of the Church in its teaching office, to Scripture as the divine criterion and norm of Christian truth.

Another noteworthy feature of the World Congress presentations was their emphasis on the universality of the Christian religion coupled with an express repudiation of universal salvation. In the recent past, modernism, influenced by evolutionary naturalism, surrendered the reality of special revelation and miraculous redemption, and in consequence, the uniqueness of Christianity. And while neo-orthodoxy insisted on Christianity as the only redemptive revelation, in its Barthian form the outcome of divine grace pointed toward universalism. Existentialist theology has also espoused universalism; moreover, its insistence that the divine-human confrontation is an encounter by God through Christ is so manifestly an intrusion of an objective claim into a subjectivistic relationship that nobody need be surprised that existentialism worked itself free of this Christocentric element, and made the universal significance of Christianity a matter of private conviction only.

Evangelical Christianity has always insisted on the universality of the Christian religion: the Living God has scripturally published the standards by which mankind will be judged, and Jesus Christ is the only saving name. But in recent years some chinks have now and then appeared in the armor of evangelical theology in regard to the lost condition of the heathen. In part such reservations—admittedly by small segments of the evangelical community—have sprung from one-sided modernist emphases on the love of God, emphases which proceed beyond the assertion that all men will share in the salvation of a loving God, to the assertion that only an unjust and unloving God could condemn those who have never even heard the Gospel. This gives rise to a type of argument that some non-Christians, living up to the light they have, will be numbered among the redeemed—Socrates for example. This argument also conditions one's views of non-Biblical religions. Syncretistic spokesmen not only assign higher and independent values to the non-Christian religions, but tend increasingly to disparage evangelistic and missionary effort; they even depict evangelicals as speaking only negatively of all religions but Christianity.

Some religion reporters for secular newspapers were especially interested in questions related to these issues, particularly so in view of recent publicity for a new attitude of Roman Catholics toward non-Christian religions. If by this altered view it is thought that Rome now concedes a saving value to non-Christian religions then one can confidently say that its position is misunderstood.

In the light of these issues it is interesting that the Berlin Congress opened with an emphasis on both general revelation and special revelation. The opening address (see appendix: "Facing a New Day in Evangelism") affirmed that the *Logos* illumines all men, that all men universally are sinners in view of their revolt against light, that redemption is to be found only in saving rescue by the incarnate *Logos,* and this on condition of personal faith. The fact that some men have never heard the Gospel is not definitive of their lost condition; it is man's revolt against light, universally, that constitutes him a sinner. The proffer of the Gospel does, indeed, offer a prospect of redemption—but of those to whom it is offered only a minority respond. Decisive for man's condemnation is what he does with the light he has—whether it includes the Gospel offer or not. The Gospel, however, remains the only way of redemption.

If the *Logos* does indeed light every man, as evangelical theology insists in keeping with the New Testament, then it is futile to contend that non-Christian religions are to be explained only in terms of darkness. The very fact that human history is invariably religious history (even when professedly anti-religious) is due to man's unique relation to the spiritual world and to his response to its claim. Not only may there be varying degrees of value in the non-

Christian religions when they are judged in terms of outward morality, but in the modern struggle against atheistic
communism they may also present possibilities of common
thought and action in promoting transcendent justice and
humanitarian concern on the part of all theistic religions.
But Judaism stands in a different relationship to Christianity than do the non-Biblical religions; the Jew has the
special light of the Old Testament, and since to him was
the Gospel first preached, Christians ought not overlook
an evangelistic interest in Jewry. But lacking above everything else in all non-Christian religions is the redemption
that is in Christ Jesus, the reality of special redemptive
revelation given in the Judeo-Christian saving events and
sacred Scriptures. That is why the Gospel must be proclaimed to the ends of the earth.

Not only does evangelical theology insist on the universality of the Christian religion, on the ground that Christ
is the Lord of creation, the King of truth, and the only
Redeemer, but it also explicitly repudiates universalism.
The notion that every human being will eventually enter
into eternal bliss has advanced, in the past century, as
James I. Packer of Latimer House, Oxford, remarks from
the status "of an idiosyncrasy to that of a respectable theological option, and it continues to make great strides
throughout the Protestant world." The remarkable thing
about the newer theories of universalism is that they profess
to advance the cause of evangelism rather than to destroy
it; some of its champions in fact hold influential posts in
the evangelistic agencies of large denominations. While
Emil Brunner rejected the universalism implicit in Karl
Barth's view that all men are divinely elected and redeemed
in Jesus Christ, and need only to know this first-hand,
Brunner himself contended for a second-chance theory
whereby those who do not accept Christ in this life will be
given further opportunity in the next. In a study book

commissioned by the World Council of Churches, D. T. Niles deplores the teaching that some will finally reject Christ as "a speculation to which the New Testament does not lend itself" and disowns the premise that "genuine and urgent conviction about the mission of the Church" requires the view that some will be damned (*Upon the Earth,* pp. 90 ff.). The recent theological undergirding differs somewhat from that in previous generations. Whereas the emphasis once fell on the dignity and perfectibility of human nature, the stress now falls on the goodness of God. As Dr. Packer notes, the newer advocates of universalism rest their case on a supposedly "irresistible theological inference" from the "overall" thrust of New Testament thinking about God. Frequently it is argued that Christ is Lord of all, and hence Saviour of all; any single exception to universalism is viewed, therefore, as a limitation and reflection on the lordship of Christ. In conformity with this view, hell itself is transformed from the ultimate state of the lost into a means of grace—a neo-Protestant purgatory of sorts.

The World Congress took explicit recognition of such theories in its declaration that "Christ is Lord of all, and Saviour of all who put their trust in Him," thus rejecting the inference from Christ's lordship to universal salvation.

While the newer theories preserve the necessity of decision, in contrast with earlier modernist theories that made universal salvation an automatic concomitant of evolutionary progress, they nonetheless render the outcome inevitable by denying that righteousness is the core of God's being and by reducing divine justice to an aspect of divine love. Recent universalism reaches beyond a secular evolutionary guarantee to a redemptive ingredient, by contending that Jesus so conquered the powers of death and resurrection that men everywhere will inevitably be included in this victory.

Dr. Packer notes that while the newer theories of universalism do not repudiate evangelism, their proponents tend to consider evangelizing others as less urgent than other expressions of love for neighbor, inasmuch as they reject the possibility of man's final doom. For all their emphasis on the importance of personal decision, the newer views sharply reduce the importance of personal commitment from its Biblical significance. It is true, of course, that in the Bible the decision or decree of God holds priority over man's decision, so that man's decision is not ultimately determinative. Redemption is God's offer, not man's devising. But according to the Bible, man's decision for Christ nonetheless changes the objective situation that prevails between God and the individual sinner. To contend, as some recent universalist theories do, that reconciliation already prevails for all men, and that each needs only to be made aware of this condition, actually does violence to the teaching of the New Testament. Man's decision for Christ does, of course, involve a knowledge of God's saving deeds and an historical redemption accomplished by Jesus Christ; faith does involve an experiential transition from "not knowing" to "knowing." But the narrowing of the significance of decision to individual awareness is due to a causal-deterministic theory of redemption that oversimplifies and distorts the dynamics of salvation. The danger of unbelief lies not simply in a delayed awareness of an inevitable redemption; it involves, in truth, the possible forfeiture of redemption. The New Testament connects unbelief not with ignorance of salvation but with divine condemnation. Election and reconciliation are not linked in a manner that makes faith merely informative, but there is an awesome connection between man's faith and the factuality of his salvation. The New Testament emphasis on "except ye believe" and "whosoever" assesses unbelief as a greater peril than does universalism. Faith not simply illumines, but is also the instrument of justification. The means of grace are significant not only for the understanding of salvation, but also for its transmission and reception. G. C. Berkouwer rightly points out that the decision of faith is not inevitably assured by man's encounter with revelation (cf. Hebrews 4:2, "the message did not benefit them, because it did not mix with faith in the hearers") ; condemnation remains an eternal possibility (cf. John 3:36, "He who does not obey the Son shall not see life, but the wrath of God rests upon him"; John 5:29, "They that have done evil [shall come forth] to the resurrection of judgment").

The theological crisis today, therefore, bears on every significant frontier of contemporary intellectual engagement, both secular and religious. The ferment of ideas in the modern world places new demands upon Evangelical Christianity for a bold and competent articulation of the Christian interpretation of life and reality.

When one speaks of the theological crisis facing evangelicals, however, it would be wrong to think only of the conflict with non-evangelical views. For at its deepest level the theological crisis is internal to the evangelical movement. In an age when church renewal is widely promoted in the absence of theological renewal, evangelicals are virtually forfeiting their opportunity to share a great revival of theological learning. The time has long passed when concentration on evangelism and missions was a necessary reaction to modernism. The failure of evangelicals to take the initiative theologically no longer indicates simply that they are strategically on the defensive because of a temporary religious situation; rather, it now raises a question over the present attitude and ability of evangelical forces. The whole ecumenical dialogue calls for bold and open theological discussions. Many Roman Catholic scholars are now open to consultations with evangelicals; in fact, to compensate for lack of familiarity with contemporary non-Catholic theology, Rome has reportedly encouraged 200 young priests to study in Protestant seminaries. Some Jewish scholars are now also interested in exchanging views with evangelicals.

But what is the theological situation among evangelicals, who insist that theology remains queen of the sciences in a day when it is widely disdained as a serf?

Are the theology departments in our evangelical seminaries and colleges centers of constructive and creative leadership amid the intellectual ferment of our day? Has there come from any of our established evangelical institutions, however prestigious, a work for our times comparable to James Orr's *A Christian View of God and the World* at the turn of the century, or to J. Gresham Machen's *The Origin of Paul's Religion* a generation ago? Where is the great theological literature that is so indispensable in a time of exploding frontiers of knowledge? Where are the theologians? Apart from J. Oliver Buswell Jr.'s two-volume *A Systematic Theology of the Christian Religion,* what systematic theology has appeared in recent decades? Not even the largest denomination in American Christianity, the Southern Baptist Convention, with its numerous seminaries and universities, has produced a systematic theology to update W. T. Conner or E. Y. Mullins. In the American Baptist Convention the situation is comparable; no contemporary replacement has appeared for A. H. Strong's three-volume *Systematic Theology.* For non-evangelical movements of religious thought, systematic theology is largely an interest of past generations, but evangelicals rally energetically to its defense. Then why not to its production?

Not only theology, but also exegetical study of the Bible remains a central concern. Doubtless considerable serious Bible study characterizes evangelical institutions today and the continuing production of learned commentaries contrasts favorably with the paucity of comprehensive theological literature. But what is happening to evangelical preaching and to Bible study in the Sunday schools and in so-called Bible conferences? How deep is the interest among laymen in more than a surface theological knowledge?

If Evangelical Christianity is to become a strong intellectual force in the closing third of the twentieth century it must aspire to theological renewal and bring itself effectively under the Word of God in the correlation of Christian conviction with all the currents of modern learning. An Institute for Advanced Christian Studies, recently proposed by *Christianity Today,* could be a helpful step toward serious theological engagement. But every evangelical seminary and college needs to be called afresh to theological earnestness and Biblical studies, and young men rallied to a theological career as a divine vocation. A movement that prizes the importance of theology cannot be intellectually influential without great theologians, and without literary publication their impact is greatly restricted. Laymen must be encouraged to read Christian thought journals, and not simply devotional literature, and the pulpit must be recaptured for a high tradition of comprehensive and compelling expository preaching.

The evangelical movements of our time have tended to be gun-shy of sustained theological engagement. The American Council of Christian Churches has had almost no positive program; its polemics are directed toward almost everything and everyone unidentified with that movement, and its theological ingredient consists mainly of an organizational salute to the fundamentalist tradition. The National Association of Evangelicals has shaped a positive program, in terms of which it can justify its existence over and above a protest against non-evangelical emphases by the National Council of Churches. But the N.A.E. also has neglected theological engagement in depth, and its recent encouragement of a theological commission has come far too late to permeate the movement as such with theological vitality. Across the years Arminian and Calvinistic elements have lived at peace for evangelical non-theological objectives in a generation when those goals were imperiled by modernist, neo-orthodox and secular ecclesiasticism. When theological engagement was ventured, its concerns were broad rather than deep, and to this day tend to revolve mainly around the central issues of the modernist-fundamentalist controversy of an earlier generation.

There is, of course, no basis for a "movement theology" —whether N.A.E. or A.C.C.C.—if one truly seeks Biblical renewal, since the truth of the Bible must in the last analysis judge all movements rather than serve merely as their adjunct or even as their basis. One main weakness of the World Council of Churches is its readiness to use theology to bolster conciliar ecumenism. Another, of course, is its patent pluralism. Still another is the continuing visibility for deviational modern views in contrast to the frequent invisibility of historical evangelical views in the theological dialogue.

What the evangelical community now specially needs is competent theological dedication and leadership. If it takes seriously the fact that the modern world is in the midst of a struggle not only for the wills of men, but also for the minds of men—indeed, for the whole man, who is called by the truth of revelation to new being in Christ—then no time must be lost in rededication to the great theological concerns which in the Protestant Reformation gave rise to Calvin's *Institutes,* Luther's *Commentaries,* Melanchthon's *Loci,* and Zwingli's *Commentary on the True and False Religion.*

CHAPTER THREE

Evangelicals and the Evangelistic Crisis

Principal James Denney noted a generation ago that evangelism had become "the disinterested interest of the comparative few." If modern Christianity had distorted the theology of the Bible, no less had it defected from the apostolic mission to the world. For the New Testament Church expected, practiced and experienced evangelism as a normal expression and barometer of its vitality. Evangelism issued effortlessly from that community of believers as light from the sun, as Richard C. Halverson, executive director of International Christian Leadership, has stated. "It was automatic, spontaneous, continuous, contagious." This vigor, moreover, issued not from external programming and organization but rather, as Halverson adds, from "repentance and healing and nurture. Because of its spiritual health"—a challenge to our condition today —"the apostolic church experienced exciting and effective evangelistic results with monotonous regularity."

Many of our modern approaches to evangelism, geared, as we like to say, to the modern needs of modern man, are in truth far removed from the Biblical concept. *Time* magazine (May 14, 1965) has noted: "The new approach to evangelism—visible in such unstructured ministries as coffee-homes, industrial missions, and missions to drag strips, ski resorts and 'night people'—is primarily interested not in selling Christianity but in sympathetically expressing a human concern for others." Evangelical dissatisfaction with such efforts is not provoked by their altruistic concern. After all, New Testament evangelism was accompanied by an unparalleled love for humanity; moreover, the evangelical message of the Cross stands as the indisputable source of humanitarian compassion in Western culture. The evangelical complaint, in a word, is that the new evangelism abridges or deletes the *evangel*—the good news of God's proffer of personal salvation and new life in Christ on the ground of the Redeemer's mediatorial death and bodily resurrection. It is not only a marked disinclination to "sell Christiaity" that defines these new approaches; it is rather a readiness to combine supposedly Christian evangelism with any and every variety of unBiblical theology, and even to detach this activity from the New Testament offer of personal participation in the redemption that is in Christ Jesus—that is, from the very *evangel* proclaimed by the apostles.

This isolation of evangelism from the New Testament evangel, and a replacement of spiritual-redemptive evangelism by secular-political "evangelism," is clearly evident in the recent re-definition of the Church's task in the world. The mission of the Church, we are now told, is the revolutionizing of social structures, not the salvation of sinners. In this exchange the ecclesiastical reluctance to "sell Christianity" yields instead to an aggressive promotion of socialism by direct involvement of the institutional Church in political power structures.

The unhappy distortion of evangelism in the modern religious scene is therefore no longer simply a matter of the use of dubious gimmicks and objectionable techniques that may manipulate human emotion—a criticism levelled at mass evangelism in the past by both foes and friends of the Gospel. The declension of Biblical evangelism is now such that hard-won Christian funds are used even to side-track and to undercut evangelism of the apostolic type. Not simply the *form* of evangelism but, as Maurice Ray suggests, the very *principle* of evangelism is now assailed, even if the verbal description is retained and subsequently applied to a type of socio-political activity by the official Church for which no scriptural precedent can be adduced. This secularizing of evangelism, no longer only by a few deviant mavericks within the institutional Church, but even by leaders specifically entrusted with the formulation of evangelistic policies and implementation of evangelistic practices in major churches, calls forth Harold John Ockenga's verdict that evangelism is now suffering from the uncertainty of its presumed friends: "The need for evangelism is denied and the nature of evangelism is misunderstood."

For Evangelical Christianity this debate over the definition of evangelism does not reduce simply to a matter of ideological contrasts. It would gravely underestimate the differences between evangelicals and nonevangelicals to concede, to be specific, that only the nature of authentic evangelism is in debate, and that no question whatever is involved concerning the adequacy of Christian love, when *agape* is thus assimilated to the secular reinterpretation of evangelism. For wherever the New Testament epistles speak of God's love for mankind, they invariably focus attention on Christ's death, that is, on the divine provision of atonement which makes possible the sinner's personal forgiveness and new life in Christ. And apostolic compassion for the world of men had at its very heart the aggressive and undiluted proclamation of this prospect of individual redemption through faith in the crucified and risen Redeemer. The conflict of the Christian apostles with Jewish and Gentile leaders controlling the political power centers of their day took place not because the Church as an organized body sought to revolutionize the established social structures, nor did it directly attack them, despite the gruesome fact of the crucifixion of Jesus Christ. It was provoked rather when those in power tried to thwart and to prohibit the apostolic preaching of Jesus Christ as the only saving Name, as the sole ground of personal salvation. To political efforts to frustrate the open proclamation of the Gospel the apostles countered with the New Testament's only revolutionary declaration: "We ought to obey God rather than man." Their driving passion was obedience to Christ's Great Commission: to proclaim the good news and to make personal disciples; their passion was not to engage the Church as a corporate body in political action aimed at restructuring social and political forms.

From this New Testament point of view, it would be a supreme act of lovelessness on the part of the Christian community to withhold from the body of humanity, lost in sin, the evangel that Christ died for sinners and that the new birth—without which no man can see the kingdom of God—is available on the condition of personal repentance and faith. This fact is of basic importance. For if the suppression of this evangel is an act of shocking lovelessness, Evangelical Christians must reject liberal and secular appeals to *agape* that redefine evangelism in terms of political involvement and social revolution, as a conscious and deliberate alternative to the divine offer of personal spiritual and moral redemption. If the New Testament is to be trusted at all, such appeals—however they may float the banner of *agape*—essentially cut off the very lifeblood of the *evangel,* namely, that Christ died and rose again for sinners.

Not only in view of the fixed New Testament foundations of the Christian faith, but also against the background of deviant currents of modern ecclesiastical speculation, we must note the special significance of the definition of evangelism derived from the World Congress on Evangelism. It reads:

"Evangelism is the proclamation of the Gospel of the crucified and risen Christ, the only Redeemer of men, according to the Scriptures, with the purpose of persuading condemned and lost sinners to put their trust in God by receiving and accepting Christ as Saviour through the power of the Holy Spirit, and to serve Christ as Lord in every calling of life and in the fellowship of His Church, looking toward the day of His coming in glory."

It is instructive to place this definition alongside an earlier, and highly serviceable one, formulated in England in 1918 by the Archbishop's Committee on Evangelism:

"To evangelize is so to present Christ Jesus in the power of the Holy Spirit, that men shall come to put their trust in God through Him, to accept Him as their Saviour and serve Him as their King in the fellowship of His Church."

This definition has preserved New Testament perspectives so fully that Evangelist Billy Graham has frequently quoted it with approval.

Yet the theological tide has drifted so far from the evangelical moorings common in the forepart of the twentieth century that the 1918 definition seemed less than fully serviceable to many participants in the World Congress on Evangelism. The Berlin formulation marks an advance over the 1918 formulation in several significant respects.

1. The 1966 definition more obviously stresses the sole mediatorship of Jesus Christ as "the only Redeemer of men."

2. It emphasizes the hopeless condition of men outside of Christ: evangelism seeks to persuade "condemned and lost sinners" to accept Christ as Savior and to serve Him as Lord. In an earlier section the Berlin declaration affirms that "All men stand under the same divine condemnation and all must find justification before God in the same way: by faith in Christ, Lord of all and Savior of all who put their trust in Him." This latter wording specifically excludes contemporary forms of universalism, which assert that since Christ is Lord of all, He is Savior of all.

3. It states more explicit the substitutionary death and resurrection of Christ for sinners. The Gospel centers in "the crucified and risen Christ, the only Redeemer of men, according to the Scriptures." Following the 1966 definition of evangelism is a statement that affirms "the good news of salvation through His atoning death and resurrection."

4. The Congress definition keeps in view the eschatological hope of the Church, the return of Jesus Christ in glory.

5. The evangelistic task is defined in context as requiring Christ's disciples to penetrate the world, rather than to withdraw from it: "Our Lord Jesus Christ, possessor of all authority in heaven and on earth, has not only called us to Himself; He has sent us out into the world to be His witnesses." Thus the secular contention is implicitly rejected that only socio-political engagement by the corporate Church preserves Christian involvement, and explicitly rejected is any effort to combine New Testament evangelism with withdrawal from society.

6. The specific and clear connection of the Gospel—in respect to both its content and proclamation—to the inspired Scriptures has been noted in an earlier chapter. It is "the crucified and risen Christ, the only Redeemer of men, according to the Scriptures" that the Gospel proclaims. Here the phrasing of the Berlin affirmation ob-

viously recalls Paul's statement of Christian fundamentals as given in I Corinthians 15:1-4.

Scarcely could it be made more obvious, therefore, in contrast to recent deviant views of evangelism that have gained favor and prestige in the National Council of Churches and World Council of Churches, that (a) the *evangel* is God's offer of individual forgiveness and of new spiritual life on the ground of the atoning death and resurrection of Jesus Christ; (b) *evangelism* is the proclamation of this gracious offer of reconciliation to persons; (c) salvation requires personal faith in Jesus Christ, the only Redeemer; (d) the Church's ultimate hope is eschatological, that is, in the personal return of Jesus Christ in glory; (e) the Church, by the personal devotion of its members to those revealed standards of righteousness by which God will judge the world, is to be the penetrating, preserving salt of society.

Stated negatively, (a) the Gospel is not reducible to social idealism; (b) social structures cannot be objects of evangelism; (c) men do not share automatically in Christ's redemptive work; (d) the Kingdom of God cannot be equated with the highest potentialities of secular history; (e) the Church as a corporate body must not rely on Caesar's sword or on legislative compulsion to advance sectarian practices.

Besides delineating this explicit definition of the Gospel the World Congress gave itself also to fully probing the strategy and the theology of evangelism.

One largely neglected door of Christian service and evangelism which Berlin swung open as an urgent opportunity is that of literacy-evangelism. Most Christian workers hear with surprise and shock that half of the adults in the late twentieth century world—almost one billion—can neither read nor write. Caught amid the world pressures of a communist-anticommunist age, the developing nations encompass hundreds of millions of illiterates and hungry "have-nots" whom propagandists readily exploit for any cause. In Russia and in Red China, and even in Cuba, communists have promoted controlled literacy campaigns that indoctrinate the masses in their ideological objectives. While Christian theology in the Western world is often cast in formulations so intricate and abstruse that only professional theologians find them intelligible, Chinese communists have simplified the language and now supply the masses with large quantities of simply-written booklets and periodicals. To the starving illiterates this new world of words and bread is more than welcome. In his new book *Reaching the Silent Billion,* Dr. David Mason, associate director of Laubach Literacy, Inc., warns that materialistic ideologists have increasingly made a special target of these restless millions; the Christian Church, he stresses, dare not forfeit half the adult world.

In literacy work Christianity has the matchless heritage of the simple profundity of Jesus Christ, of the Bible as the Book of the Ages, and of pioneering Christian missions that challenge suppression and superstition. Since 40,000 Bible-teaching Christian missionaries are already at work in nations where illiteracy is a serious problem, and millions of national Christians can be enlisted in these lands, literacy evangelism could well be a superlative opportunity of reaching adults. People respond by the hundreds wherever they are offered instruction in reading, and even lands that now exclude missionaries in the traditional sense welcome them as literacy specialists. The expanding effort of Laubach Literacy, provision of in-service training in mission compounds, summer institutes or workshops for furloughed missionaries, and Christian college or seminary courses in techniques of literacy evangelism can all contribute hopefully to this frontier work. Christian editors are duty-bound to inform the Christian world of this need and opportunity; Christian educators have the duty to prepare students in the techniques of literacy work; Christian evangelists must take the Word of Life to those who now are strangers to the world of words.

If the restless world of illiterates supplies a dramatic and too-long-neglected opportunity for evangelism, the newly-literate masses also provide a strategic field. They must not be left without the Bible and without other Christian literature suited to their learning needs. In fact, literature evangelism has become one of the foremost means of influencing both the literate and illiterate worlds. Martin Luther said, "God's supreme gift to Christendom to aid the spread of the gospel is the printing press." Jack McAlister of World Literature Crusade rightly contends that the facts of a burgeoning population require the use of mass media literature if the whole world is to be confronted by the Gospel. Evangelical Christianity must now learn how to convey spiritual and moral truth to the multitudes whose daily reading consists of large-circulation secular newspapers or of best-selling novels, who seldom if ever see a religious magazine and, in any event, would consider it an oddity. Someone recently noted that while evangelical influence is minimal in French-speaking Africa, contrary to what one might hope, French-speaking Protestants in Europe and Canada have had no proportionate evangelistic interest despite their greater numbers. The neglect of journalism and creative writing as a means of Christian influence is a staggering indictment of the prevalent sense of vocational values. Too little evangelical literary talent is available, and much of what is available is preoccupied with non-literary demands or pursuits. Evangelical circles have too much duplication of literary effort; certain magazines, for example, could be effectively merged, or their reason for being might profitably be re-examined. At the present time surveys of religious literature show that by far the largest percentage of evangelical copy is directed toward pastors, a small percentage toward laymen, and a negligible percentage toward the unevangelized millions. Dayton Roberts acknowledges that only 4 per cent of the literature produced by Latin American Mission, one of the most effective evangelical agencies, is directed toward non-Christians. Moreover, magazine publication has become increasingly expensive, especially if it incorporates contemporary techniques. In the United States, in fact, no religious periodical of any significance can survive without subsidy either by denominational or individual sources.

Perhaps the largest single opportunity in the American religious magazine field is for a weekly newsmagazine similar to *Time* that carries interpretative essays on spiritual and moral concerns. It is unlikely, however, that sufficient advertising can be garnered to insure the financial stability of such an effort. While Evangelical Christians forego this opportunity, the probability increases that the giant mergers of major denominations into the conciliar movement may result in replacing church journals with a monolithic newsmagazine promotive of conciliar concerns and subsidized by ecumenical funds. The fact that publications of N.C.C.-affiliated denominations have increasingly emphasized ecumenical perspectives may be viewed as ideologically preparatory for a journal of theologically pluralistic emphasis.

But the largest opportunity today is in the secular mainstream of journalism. In a single issue the great daily newspapers and the national-circulation magazines reach more persons than many clergymen reach in an entire lifetime. The religious message that is effectively shaped for reception by the uncommitted masses must meet the first test of communication on radio, television and film, no less than on the printed page. The messenger who writes for the uncommitted must, in Bishop A. W. Goodwin Hudson's words, "bring religious phraseology into the language of ordinary un-theological men and women." In the public press the crowd is ready-made.

Even on a commercial advertising basis the big-city dailies offer direct access to huge multitudes. If a young Christian were to dedicate his life to mastering the effective communication of ideas, and a group of believers were to underwrite a full page of copy even just several times a year, the results could be enormous. In England for $2,000 one can buy a whole page of space in a newspaper that has 3½ million readers. In the United States the three largest daily newspapers likewise provide mass circulation access at a cost of less than a half cent per person based on a one-time black-and-white full page rate of $4,380 in the *New York News,* a tabloid with 2,100,000 circulation; $4,-800 in the *Los Angeles Times,* with 845,000 circulation; and $4,791 in the *Chicago Tribune,* also with 845,000 circulation. What if another C. S. Lewis were to engage his own particular generation in this way?

But no less influential can be the skilled journalist who knows how to focus on the religious and moral forces of our time and how to mirror these in irresistible copy. Jan J. van Capellevan, religion editor of *Rotterdamer* in The Netherlands, reminds us that "Communicating the Gospel means not only preaching a message, but also telling what God is doing in our own time. . . . He who has seen what God has done, can better comprehend what God wants." If in twenty years, as some predict, technology will enable a person to pick up his 48-page daily newspaper by pressing a television button, the role of the effective religion reporter will be all the more critical.

Among the convictions that settled over the World Congress was the realization that to neglect mass media and modern scientific aids for evangelizing the earth is a

sin for which twentieth century Christians might well be
held especially responsible. Using these tools does not
mean attempting to convert men by reliance on gimmicks
and projects including Madison Avenue promotional techniques, for it is the Holy Spirit alone who gives new life,
and who enables individuals to decide for Christ in response
to the good news of redemption. There must be open recognition, however, that contemporary Christians dare not
try to work and witness for God as if they still lived in "a
pre-radio, pre-television, pre-electronic era." Bishop Hudson rightly reminds us that "We cannot think of the Great
Reformation without the use of the printing press. And
the first use given to this invention was the printing of
the Bible. . . . It might be debated," he adds, "whether any
revival of true religion has ever come without the use of
modern means of communication." Both Adolf Hitler and
Winston Churchill stirred their nations for different pur-
poses by an effective use of radio and television. Today
radio and television are gaining global importance; as never
before electronic and mass media techniques exert a massive materialistic influence on people practically everywhere. Is the use of such means to be abandoned to tyrants,
secularists, and deviant theologians who advocate a "new
morality" or proclaim the death of God? Dr. Oswald C. J.
Hoffmann remarks that "in an age of developing dialogue
where none existed before, new doors seem to be opening
for genuine dialogue with people through the use of mass
media." Dr. Billy Graham reports that proportionately
more people will respond to the Gospel on television than
to any other means of communication. Yet although television has been a reality for three decades, it remains a
strange new medium for most Christian leaders.

Two groups in modern society are critically important
in today's world. One is comprised of the inhabitants of
the giant metropolises. "If we can conquer the great cities

of the world with the Gospel," says Akira Hatori of Tokyo, the world's largest city, "we can extend that victory and impact to the rest of the nation, and more than that, to the rest of the world." Tokyo alone has 11 million inhabitants; by 2000 A.D., according to estimates, its population will be 30 million, and the 200 miles from Tokyo to Nagoya will constitute one vast metropolis. And in India it is estimated that about twenty cities will each have 20 million inhabitants. The rise of such great megapolises, their inhabitants sealed off in concrete jungles or huge apartment complexes, requires vigilant use of mass media, and alert pursuit of personal relationships. Ross Hidy notes that the early apostles aimed at the large Mediterranean cities as strategic targets. Today's cities are often centers of loneliness and vice, of commercialism and slums and ghettos. The spiritual fate of these cities could very well be decisive for the impact of the Gospel in the next generation.

There is a second sector of humanity, however, upon whose Christian or non-Christian commitment may depend the virility of Biblical religion in the remainder of this century. That is the student world. The number of university students is now almost 20 million, many of whom will fill places of leadership in the years ahead. Says Eric Fife, missionary secretary of Inter-Varsity Christian Fellowship: "University students today live in a spiritual vacuum. . . . In ten years' time these are the people who will be editing your newspapers . . . producing your television programs . . . running or ruining your countries." The leaders of the Protestant Reformation, Luther, Calvin, Zwingli, Melanchthon, and so on, were all university-trained scholars. Today's mounting emphasis on university learning makes imperative a special interest in the campus world. Christ must be presented as the answer to the vacuum in the lives of students and Christianity as the solution to their intellectual problems. The time is propitious for a great World Student Congress; it could enlist evangelical faculty and student resources for an intellectual and moral offensive for the Gospel in the closing decades of the twentieth century.

If the World Congress at Berlin was concerned with the definition and strategy of evangelism, no less was it confronted with questions of method.

Dr. José Martinez of Barcelona, Spain, has cautioned that any emphasis on methods runs the risk of elevating techniques to disproportionate importance, "as if the ultimate success of the proclamation of the Gospel depended upon them. . . . Christians filled with the Holy Spirit will always find an effective way to evangelize. But the best systems will fail if the power of the Holy Spirit is lacking." It might be said that all methods that declare God's Word can be legitimately employed, and that a Church lacking any method whatever of proclaiming the Gospel can only be a disobedient Church. The anecdote may exaggerate the realities of the case, but Professor Daniel Bakhsh of West Pakistan tells a story that makes its point against excessive timidity. When a teen-ager asked his athletic coach how to ask a girl for a date, the coach replied: "Son, there is no wrong way to do it." The speaker of the Lutheran Hour, Dr. Oswald C. J. Hoffmann, has appropriately warned against canonizing "any one method of evangelism." Dr. Horace F. Fenton similarly notes that too often Christians isolate one method from all others; sometimes a lamentable rivalry and competition arises between agencies and movements predicated simply on differences of methodology.

The contrast of individual and mass evangelism is often rigidly exaggerated, for whether contemplated from the standpoint of theory or practice, the difference between them is only relative and not absolute. While individuals may be addressed either alone or in a group, all effective evangelism in the final analysis must be personal. The goal of evangelism is to reach the world, that is, the great mass of unregenerate humanity, for individual commitment to Christ. Twenty years ago many churchmen solemnly announced that the day of mass evangelism was gone. But the spectacular world-wide ministry of Evangelist Billy Graham, who has preached the Gospel to more millions than anyone in history, has long discredited such dour prophecies, although an echo of them is occasionally heard even today. While special methods may be appropriate to particular groups, Dr. James R. Graham emphasizes, quite rightly, that in apostolic times priority for hearing Christ's Gospel "rested not on wealth, position, power, influence or education" but the good news was proclaimed "to the cross-section of society wherever the message had not penetrated: 'Jerusalem . . . all Judea . . . Samaria . . . the uttermost part. . . .' "

Yet a one-sided reliance on mass evangelism through large crusades can be self-defeating if it concentrates interest primarily in the ministry of a few prominent evangelists. Dr. Walter H. Smyth, director of crusades for the Billy Graham Evangelistic Association, has remarked that if Graham were to accept his entire backlog of invitations, it would take the evangelist 200 years to fulfill them, and Graham himself has mentioned that he probably will not be able to continue his present energetic pace of activity for more than ten years.

Besides big-city crusades such as those associated with Graham's ministry there are a variety of other successful approaches for reaching the masses. In Latin America, Evangelism-in-Depth has coordinated the resources and methods of many agencies for simultaneous, cooperative evangelism. Since 1960 seven nations have felt its impact: Nicaragua, Costa Rica, Guatemala, Honduras, Venezuela,

Bolivia and the Dominican Republic; Peru and Colombia are targets for 1967 and 1968 respectively. Evangelism-in-Depth's comprehensive strategy includes prayer cells, training believers in soul-winning, local house-to-house visitation, specialized visitation by and to vocational groups, various smaller evangelistic meetings that culminate in a national campaign in the capital city, and a follow-up continuation program. In many American cities simultaneous crusades by cooperating churches are proving more effective than individual church efforts. Among the dividends of mass evangelism by cooperating evangelical churches, says Gregorio Tingson of Manila, is the "welding" of "a more cohesive evangelical testimony which, in turn, enlarges the evangelistic vision of the cooperating evangelical groups." Dr. C. E. Autrey, long director of the Division of Evangelism of the Southern Baptist Convention, reports that the simultaneous crusade was the major method employed by Southern Baptists between 1954 and 1964 in winning and baptizing 4,334,000 persons. In the 1969 Crusade of the Americas projected by Southern Baptists, evangelical churches of whatever denominational affiliation will have opportunity to cooperate on a city-wide basis.

The crisis in evangelism as it exists for evangelical Christianity today, however, is at its deepest level neither a crisis of definition nor one of method. It is a crisis of engagement. In an article captioned "What is the Issue in Christianity Today?" in the *Church Herald* (October 22, 1965), I stressed that the torchbearers are vanishing, and noted that the ultimate issue now facing the Church is whether Biblical Christianity will be effectively communicated to the oncoming generation. To this question Evangelical Christians can reply only by their devotion to the Great Commission, for the present decline of evangelistic compassion is the most crucial concern facing Christendom today. In the apostolic age believers were far less numerous than we, and beset with their share of perversions of the Gospel. Nonetheless that "company of the committed," to borrow Elton Trueblood's apt description, gave itself unreservedly to the joyous ministry of reconciliation.

Evangelist Leo Janz of Switzerland contends that today "only five per cent of all Christians ever directly lead another person to Christ." What this trend implies for the future of Christianity, if it is unarrested and unreversed, is clear when one realizes how much swifter and more numerous is the increase of the world's population than of those who accept Christ. The shocking fact that the non-witnessing believers actually aid and abet the paganizing of the world was dramatically demonstrated to delegates of the World Congress on Evangelism. During their ten days of deliberation in the Berlin Kongresshalle, the net increase in world population, as shown by the relentlessly ticking population clock, totaled about 1,800,000. According to the Population Reference Bureau in Washington, D.C., the world's population increases an average of 2.14 persons each second, 128 each minute, 7,704 every hour, 184,896 every day. How few are being won to Christ!

On the basis of church statistics, says William R. Bright, president of Campus Crusade for Christ, it takes six pastors and one thousand laymen in the United States to introduce one person to Jesus Christ in an entire year. The impotence of twentieth century Christianity, he contends, is evidenced by the fact that many Christians today actually expect a negative response to personal witness for Christ, while in actuality multitudes are sincerely searching for a religious faith.

No doubt a case can be made from the Bible for the confidence that the ascended Lord bestows upon certain persons the distinct gift for being evangelists (cf. Ephesians) 4:8-11, "When Christ ascended up on high, he . . . gave

gifts unto men. . . . And he gave . . . some, evangelists . . .").
But nothing in the New Testament supports the notion
that evangelism is the duty only of some and not of all
followers of Christ. It is perfectly clear, moreover, that in
contrast with the current reliance on mass meetings for
the conversion of unbelievers, apostolic Christianity relied
mainly on the universal witness of individual believers. The
noun "evangelist" occurs only three times in the New
Testament, while the verb "to evangelize" is found more
than fifty times.

These New Testament facts lead to several conclusions.

Churches whose doors are closed to evangelists are bar-
ricading themselves not against men but against God and
His blessing. "Many witnesses and much activity," says
Anton Schulte, the German evangelist, "are no substitute
for the evangelist as God's gift." In the plan and purpose
of God, evangelization of the world requires men specially
endowed with this gift of evangelism; churches ought always to pray, therefore, that God will raise up His chosen
evangelists for their distinctive work.

At the same time, churches that rely wholly upon evangelists for the task of evangelism thwart God's correlative
purpose for all believers to serve personally as witnesses to
the redemption that is in Christ Jesus. True evangelism
aims, as Leighton Ford stresses, at mobilization of the laity,
and at a continuing post-campaign strategy for reaching
others. The ministry of the local church falls short of its
goal whenever the evangelized hesitate to engage in evangelism; the New Testament clearly attests that Jesus expected every disciple to witness and evangelize. Richard
Halverson says: "Evangelism in the finest New Testament
tradition is the vocation of every believer. . . . Any methodology which produces a kind of semiprofessional class of
evangelists within the Christian community, implying that
personal evangelism is limited to those who have the time

and/or inclination to take special courses and learn special methods, militates against total involvement, justifies those who default and discourages those unable to enroll for and master certain evangelistic techniques. In such a situation the distinctive feature is not one's relation to Jesus Christ, to the Holy Spirit, and to others in the Christian family, but rather an artificial 'system' which, however effectively used by its proponents, tends to make all others, voluntarily or involuntarily, feel useless so far as evangelism is concerned." The evangelistic ministry is not reserved for an élite few, for those professionally educated and equipped to evangelize, nor is it even the secular task of a semi-professional company specially indoctrinated in evangelistic techniques. Evangelism is the task of every believer. However justified lay institutes of evangelism may be, however appropriate studies of effective evangelistic techniques, they must never become a stop-gap that dilutes the evangelistic zeal of ordinary Christians by suggesting that they have been inadequately equipped by the Holy Spirit for an empowered witness to Jesus Christ.

Every twice-born church-goer today should be witnessing to his world of the transforming grace of God. If the example of Jesus is any criterion at all for us, we ought not linger unduly in the pious isolation of the temple, but rather go out and speak out to the worst and best of unregenerate men concerning new life in Christ. Jesus of Nazareth was found "among tax collectors and women of the street. The Pharisees turned up their noses at this," notes Anton Schulte, "but Jesus spoke the everyday language of the people of His time. He actually spoke Aramaic, the dialect spoken in the streets. The apostles did not write their epistles in classical Greek but in Koine. Can we still speak like an ordinary worker?" We might well ask ourselves if perhaps we have lost the ability to speak of God to our neighbors in terms of their own aspirations and longings, in words and ideas that strike home. Do not Jesus' questions—and He asks them of us all—pierce the hedonism of our affluent age and the self-indulgent morality of our society?

The first Christian witnesses, as Oral Roberts reminds us, "were positive people . . . quickened by the supernatural. . . . They took the offensive and went to the people instead of waiting for the people to come to them. They witnessed in jails, in courtrooms, in open fields, along the river banks, and on boats." ". . . The Early Church," New Zealand evangelist Muri Thompson reminds us, "seemed invincible, its attitude toward life almost irresistible in the light of the resurrection."

Today, however, many Christians witness neither to their nearest neighbors nor even to friends and relatives. They neglect the possibilities of evangelistic witness by letter. They do not even pray for the lost whose lives they touch daily.

The evangelistic crisis in evangelical circles reduces therefore to one driving question: Shall we abandon evangelism to communism and the cults, which have inherited a zeal for the unenlisted? Shall we abandon evangelism and thus deprive our generation of the good news of the Mediator who, at the Father's bidding, left the isolation of heaven for a mission to mankind, and who commissions us still for our task in the world with the reminder, "As the Father has sent me, so send I you"?

CHAPTER FOUR

Evangelicals and the Social Crisis

By divine creation man is made for life in three families
—fellowship with God, marital love in the home, and
justice in the social order.

By redemption he becomes a four-family man; he is included in the company of the redeemed. He must not, however, on that account, remove himself from the world.

Indeed, as Walter Künneth of Erlangen has said, "The
Church is not called to flee and despise the world, not
forced into narrow-minded isolation, not condemned to a
ghetto existence; just the reverse is true: The Church is
called to be on display before the world. . . . The Church
has become the beginning of 'a new creation'." The greatest weakness of evangelicals today, says John Stott is
their effort to evangelize without going *into* the world.
"We do not identify," he asserts. "We believe so strongly
(and rightly so) in proclamation, that we tend to proclaim
our message from a distance. We sometimes appear like
people who shout advice to drowning men from the safety
of the seashore. . . . But Jesus Christ did not broadcast
salvation from the sky."

Stott ascribes this reluctance partly to a "sharp reaction against certain theological liberals and radicals who lay such stress on identification that they have renounced altogether the duty to proclaim the Gospel." Indeed, in its wise rejection of the social gospel in the forepart of this century, the evangelical movement reacted to the unwise neglect of the larger social implications of the Gospel. Harold Kuhn warns that besides the damaging liberal tendency "to identify the great ecclesiastical structures with specific programs of social and economic betterment" there exists "an equally grave peril of restricting the cutting edge of the Christian evangel solely to the matter of personal redemption, and of neglecting the manner in which the Christian mandate brings the claims of the Sovereign Lord of all life to bear upon all the structures of society." Christian denial of neighbor love may in fact become an offense to the world that prevents effective hearing of the Gospel. To quote Stott again: "How can we become so one with secular men and women, as Christ became one with us, that we express and demonstrate our love for them, and win a right to share with them the good news of Christ? I am not content to shout the Gospel at them from a remote and sheltered vantage ground; I want to become their friend and argue it out with them side by side; I want to witness to Christ among them in their very midst. Just how to do this is an urgent question to which we must address ourselves seriously if we would follow in the footsteps of our Master."

Paul S. Rees, vice president of World Vision, stresses that "the confirming witness of believers is one in which they stand related to the whole of life and to the total fabric of society. . . . Nothing human is alien to their interest." If evangelicals shun the realms of politics, economics, and social order, then, as Benjamin Moraes of Brazil points out, the whole conduct of world affairs will be forfeited to others by the very persons who are called to be the salt of the earth and light of the world. Or, if evangelicals withdraw from socio-political engagement, they enable others who profess Christian social concern to promote non-evangelical programs that lack a sure connection with the principles of early Christianity.

Yet it cannot be argued that evangelicals hold an agreed position on how Christian social concern ought ideally to be ventured. There is, assuredly, increasing disapproval of what José D. Fajardo of Colombia, recalling how in his youth he was often sent out into the pasture to recover a horse, depicts as a mere "banana-halter" type of charity that approaches mankind with the banana of kindness in one hand and the halter of conversion in the other. Yet the repeated failure of liberal neo-Protestant social and political ideals to reflect Christianity authentically stirs deep reservations over the nature of justifiable involvement in public affairs. In fact, among evangelicals the social crisis includes their own necessity of somehow effectively adjusting their widening determination to break out of public isolation to an equally sincere determination to avoid the grievous errors of neo-Protestant liberalism in the social arena.

Can the evangelical vanguard in the remaining third of this century redress the liberal miscarriage of the Christian opportunity in the earlier two-thirds? At the turn of the last century James Orr, in lectures on *The Christian View of God and the World,* noted that "in our century the world is opened up as never before, and the means of a rapid spread of the Gospel are put within our power, if the Church has only faithfulness to use them. It is difficult to avoid the belief that the singular development of conditions in this century, its unexampled progress in discovery and in the practical mastery of nature, the marvelous opening up of the world which has been the result, and the extraordinary multiplication of the means and agencies of rapid communication, together portend some striking development of the Kingdom of God which shall cast all others into the shade—a crisis, perhaps, which shall have the most profound effect upon the future of humanity" (pp. 360 ff). These words are no less an apt description of our own times.

How then ought evangelicals to declare themselves in respect to the pressing social concerns of our age? The World Congress on Evangelism did not provide an answer to that question. In line with its objective, it viewed most social concerns, including such issues as the population explosion, from the standpoint of evangelistic incentive. On some key issues it doubtless provided important suggestions for the facing of social concerns. But it also reflected significant divisions within the evangelical community touching Christian responsibility at some of the major frontiers of contemporary social concern. At the same time it brought the conflict between neo-Protestant liberalism and evangelical Christianity to a new climax of antagonism over political involvement.

It has long been popular among modernist social activists to caricature evangelicals—in view of their repudiation of the social gospel—as social reactionaries, and the label has been fastened on evangelicals whether they have been socially inactive or active. A generation ago the clash between champions of miraculous theism and of secular modernism was especially evident in the area of theology; *The Christian Century,* in fact, asserted that fundamentalists and liberals were actually worshiping different gods. (When classic liberalism later collapsed, it never occurred to the *Century* to openly acknowledge that the liberals had engaged their churches in idolatry.) But by the 1960s the center of controversy had further shifted from theology to social ethics; the stance of nonevangelical Protestantism had now become so anti-metaphysical and anti-intellectual that truth was subordinated to unity, theology was widely viewed as a matter of subjective preference, and in place of an absolute dogma stood an approved program of social action which—as the liberals saw it—was now the real test of genuine Christian commitment. Instead of personal evangelism and the spiritual regeneration of individuals, they advocated changing the social structures by the Church's direct engagement in political controversy.

These differences were brought into focus in advance of the World Congress on Evangelism, in a letter in which a National Council of Churches spokesman encouraged Berlin churchmen to view the delegates attending the Congress in a category with German Christians who wanted the Church to stick to "business as usual," so that the Nazi slaughter of six million Jews would not interfere with traditional priorities. Had the Congress delegates been informed of this smear attempt, they could not have given a more obvious refutation than their own bold indictment of racism that Evangelist Billy Graham hailed as "the strongest that ever came out of a Protestant church gathering." As it was, the statement emerged as an expression of heart and conscience rather than of reaction and resentment.

Yet the London *Times* of November 5, 1966, in the same issue reporting this "blunt condemnation of racial prejudice" also carried a major essay by a special correspondent emphasizing that Christian forces are now divided over two radically different views of changing the world. World Congress denunciation of racism—reported elsewhere in the *Times*—was wholly ignored because of the obvious evangelical reliance on spiritual and regenerative dynamisms rather than on political compulsion by secular pressures of the institutional Church. Indeed, the *Times* correspondent even echoed the antipathy of some ecumenical aides in Berlin toward the Congress: "In Hitler's Germany many preachers went on proclaiming the 'pure

Gospel', which in no way disturbed the merchants of death.
But a few Christians stood by a persecuted Jew. . . . Here
are two *different* faiths." On the one side, the *Times* correspondent ranged Billy Graham as a champion of a Gospel that seeks to rescue individuals from a lost world by
personal faith in Jesus Christ as Redeemer; on the other
side, Martin Luther King, who espouses a theology and
program of "Christian revolution" that functions through
political commitment. These are "two utterly different
attitudes toward the hell that men have made of the world.
Both claim to be Christian. . . . They reflect a division in
the Church that probably goes deeper than any historic
denominational dispute. The very nature of faith is at issue.
This dispute runs right through every denomination. . . ."
(The Times, "Are religion and politics the same?,"
November 5, 1966).

It will help to clarify these tensions if we note that
liberal neo-Protestantism now not only insists that the inversion of social structures is more important than con-
verting individuals—a thesis for which its spokesmen are
indebted to Karl Marx—but also that it increasingly en-
dorses socialism in the name of Christian economics and
approves the results of social revolution as a benevolent
achievement of divine providence. The recent conference
on the Church and Society, sponsored by the World Council
of Churches, left little doubt about its sympathy for socialism and its hostility to capitalism. Evangelical Christians,
on the other hand, repudiate this attempt to confer Christian sanction on secular and often anti-Biblical ends, and
they reject revolution as an approved means of achieving
social change. The depth at which this ecclesiastical conflict
now rages is even more apparent in underground gutter
tactics that do not come into open view. When, for example, the World Congress on Evangelism sought to travel
to Wittenberg in East Germany for a Reformation Sunday

devotional service near the castle where the Reformer posted his famous 95 theses, communist authorities dangled the request interminably, after an inquiry to Geneva, head-quarters of the World Council of Churches, yielded word that the Congress would view the Council's 1966 Church and Society Conference as "too far left." World Congress officials finally scheduled their public demonstration in West Berlin rather than East Germany. If one spells out this prejudice—that socio-political attitudes should hold priority over all ecclesiastical goals—he will sense the stance of neo-liberal radicals in the World Council who increas-ingly place the more moderate liberals of recent decades on the defensive. Their position is not that socio-political engagement by the institutional Church is "more impor-tant" than evangelism, but rather that such socio-political engagement *is* evangelism, and some are personally sympa-thetic with the revolutionary overthrow of capitalism and the forced implementation of socialism.

Evangelical Christians, it should be acknowledged, often speak of Christianity as a "revolutionary religion" and of the Nazarene as "the revolutionary Jesus." What they in-tend to emphasize thereby, however, is that the Christian challenge to the existing orders of society is thorough-going and radical—more so than that posed by any ideological alternative. But this way of speaking now has definite risks of misunderstanding, because of today's predominantly com-munistic connotation of the term "revolution." Moreover, not only communists but also some ecumenical churchmen exploit the idea of "the revolutionary Christ" and of Chris-tianity as a "revolutionary" religion in order to confer ecclesiastical sanction upon Marxist economic ideas.

Hence in social ethics as in theology it is still best to pre-serve a Biblical vocabulary and meaning by speaking of regeneration rather than of revolution. There will always be those churchmen, of course, who distort even the Scriptural motifs; currently the term "conversion" is undergoing an ecumenical gyration that demands Christian conjunction with the world rather than rescue from the world. But in fact the Biblical demand for regeneration strikes deeper than rival demands for social revolution. It indicts the social sphere not only as an arena of rampant injustice and unrighteousness, but also as fallen from God's holy intention by creation, and therefore under His condemnation. Whatever improvements the proponents of revolution may achieve in the social realm, these too are defective from the standpoint of the Bible, which aims not simply at the overthrow of existing unjust structures but at the regeneration of fallen men and at the reestablishment of the divine orders of creation through observance of the scripturally revealed principles of social ethics.

In respect to human rights, the difference between these two views of man and reality becomes immediately apparent. The communist view is explicitly secular and non-supernaturalistic; it exalts the totalitarian state as the source, sanction and stipulator of all man's rights. The Christian revelation affirms God as the creator of life, and man as a creature fashioned in the divine image for intelligible obedience to God's revealed will. Both man's rights and duties have their source, sanction, and specification in the revealed will of his Maker. Civil government has a divinely intended role in a fallen society, but that role is a servant role—as a minister of justice—and not a totalitarian role as the definer of justice. Many Christian statesmen—among them John Foster Dulles—were enthusiastic over the United Nations because of its declaration of human rights (viewed as universal rather than geographical); many Christian spokesmen were equally disturbed because that declaration failed to stipulate a supernatural grounding of man's rights. The Evangelical community has often pointed out that neither the state nor a superstate (a world government or an alliance of great powers) can ultimately guarantee human rights, since wherever government is viewed as the final source of rights, man possesses no rights against government. The communist theory, moreover, is doubly objectionable: it not only suspends rights on the totalitarian state, but it also espouses an evolutionary philosophy which simply cannot sustain the case for universal and enduring rights. While the Bible does not—contrary to the classic Roman view of life and law—assert absolute human rights on the basis of man's inherent divinity, it does base human rights on the divine creation of man and the scriptural revelation of God's purpose. While man has no absolute property rights, for example, the Bible is clearly on the side of private property held as a stewardship under God. And the Christian vanguard in apostolic times, when the pagan Roman empire combined its totalitarian claims with an emphasis on the inherent human dignity and rights of its citizens, invoked those rights when necessary, as when Paul carried his appeal to Caesar, and others insisted on freedom to fulfill the Great Commission against rulers who would have silenced them.

Yet the conciliar movement and the Evangelical community today are both strangely divided over what attitude Christians should take toward social justice. In the Soviet sphere neither the World Council of Churches nor unaffiliated Evangelicals seem much concerned about human rights over against the state; in the Free World, many conciliar churchmen have become so preoccupied with human rights that this issue displaces evangelism, while Evangelical leaders are devoted to evangelism and divided over the nature of Christian socio-political duty. Since we are here concerned with Evangelicals and the social crisis, we shall attempt to assess the Evangelical situation through the World Congress on Evangelism.

In Berlin there was frequent mention of the totalitarian ideologies and their anti-Christ tendencies. Johannes Schneider spoke of the "revolt from God that culminates in political ideologies and world views tied up with atheism to the very point of enmity toward God and Christ and persecution of the church. . . . It is said, God hinders man's free development. In truth, however, when man surrenders his ties to God, he does not become really free, but plunges all the more deeply rather into the grip of Satanic-demonic powers." Samuel Escobar of Argentina pointed out that the two most notorious examples of totalitarian nationalism in the twentieth century, Nazism and communism, elevated their ideologies into a state religion and applied their collectivistic notions about the nature of man so as to deny the basic freedom of individuals. There was an awareness also of the deceptive commitment of Soviet Russia to the United Nations charter. Helen Kim, many years Korean delegate to the United Nations, declared that: "The method used to successfully block the advance of Christianity in communist countries has been both subtle and direct. Freedom of religion is guaranteed, at first, but quietly and systematically, church work in welfare agencies, hospitals, and education is banned, church literature is restricted until only worship is left, and this is usually scheduled when attendance is demanded elsewhere. The policy of communists outside of communist countries has been equally defeating. By classifying religion as 'an opiate of the people' used by 'capitalists' to keep the 'workers happy while exploited,' or by making missionaries out to be puppets of the 'imperialists,' the communists have tried to make Christian belief as unattractive outside their immediate spheres of influence as they have within." Dr. Kim, who is president emeritus of Ewha Womans University in Seoul, one of the largest universities for women in the world, added that "the pattern in all communist countries is clear: First, oppression of religion; second, divisiveness, and a militant movement of atheism; and third, use of what religion and Christianity remains for communist ends." She noted that the Soviet Union established a center for atheistic indoctrination that sponsored 239,000 meetings reaching 10,765,000 persons in a single year; while Christian literature was restricted or banned, the League of Militant Godless published 14,200,000 pieces of literature in a single year. She estimated that the number of Christian believers in Russia had been cut from 80% to 30% by 1960 through indirect pressures, persecution, and death. In North Korea between 1959 and 1960, she reported, 7,000 communist party leaders liquidated 3,000,000 persons, including all Christians, and there are presently no indications of a surviving Church. Andrew Ben Loo of Taiwan declares that 25 million is now regarded as a conservative estimate of persons liquidated by the communists in Red China, and that churches, hospitals, schools, and orphanages have been seized and confiscated. First, totalitarianism creates an anti-Christian ideological atmosphere through every means of mass communication; then the Christian community is isolated; next, the Christian witness is infiltrated, misrepresented, and perverted. Churchmen who cooperate are viewed as church leaders and are then honored with party positions. The One-Church movement is accompanied by increasing pressures in Church councils for admission of Red China to the United Nations where, says Loo, delegates from Red China would in fact represent only 5% (the communist cadres) of the 600 million population.

Viewed pragmatically, as Harold Kuhn says, the fact is that "where totalitarian systems prevail, mission fields close and evangelism, of the public variety at least, ceases." Communist antagonism to Christian evangelism is reflected in different ways: in much of Latin America communism exists mainly as a competing materialistic ideology that

seeks the same control as in Cuba over political and economic structures; in Eastern Europe, communism controls
the socio-political structures—it permits the operation of
Christian churches, but severely curtails their public evangelistic activity; in the Orient communists have ruthlessly
opposed and extirpated Christianity.

Yet if one searches the papers presented by Evangelical
Christians at the World Congress, he is caught up sharply
by the divergent attitudes toward socio-political concerns,
including Christianity's interest in human rights. Surely
the position of conciliar ecumenism today is that not only
Christians as individuals but the Church as an institution
ought to be aggressively engaged for political ends; in fact,
as we have noted, in ecumenical circles the inversion of
social structures has become more important than evangelism, and socialism has become the predominant credo.
Yet the World Council critique of governments, however
blunt in the free world, is negligible in the communist
world; the weight of official ecclesiastical opinion often
seems now to give comfort to communist aggression. Often
it is said—by conciliar ecumenists in defending their anti-
American declarations—that Evangelicals are addicted to
"American-firstism" or to reactionary capitalism, rather
than to international justice.

What then of evangelical conviction in respect to socio-
political concerns?

It is noteworthy that Josip Horak, president of the
Yugoslavian Baptist Convention, told a discussion group
at the World Congress on Evangelism: "We should not
lose our so precious time for propagating or fighting political ideas. Our job is to proclaim the Gospel of salvation
and so hasten our Lord's return. . . . Many times we
dispute at length about freedom of religion. We should
remember that dead men do not need this freedom or
other human rights. Dead Christians, nominal Christians,

do not need to be given freedom of religion—many never use the wonderful privileges they have—their freedom to evangelize, their open door to witnessing."

Horak would be first to concede that Christians in the East Zone lack many opportunities for propagating the Gospel enjoyed by believers in the Free World. "It is true, of course," he said, "that we do not have the same opportunities for evangelism as some others . . . (while) in many countries believers cannot conduct mass meetings. . . . Many methods that are highly useful in Western countries are not adequate for the present situation in many Eastern lands." From indications in the secondary movements of his paper one can gain glimpses of the restrictions on religious liberty in Yugoslavia: "(If) distribution of tracts is forbidden. . . . (If) there are no opportunities to preach in the streets. . . . (If) we cannot witness from house to house. . . . We have the special opportunity of using radio for evangelism . . . from the outside [e.g., Trans-World Radio, which sends out six weekly broadcasts in Yugoslavian from Monte Carlo and Bonaire]. . . . Thus many can be reached . . . who without radio could not be reached at all for various reasons: believers may be few in number, for example, or unbelievers may be afraid to contact believers directly."

Now all Evangelicals would consider highly appropriate Dr. Horak's rebuke to believers who do not use to the full whatever opportunities they have in the work of fulfilling the Great Commission. "In every country," he stresses, "believers have their opportunities even if perhaps their methods differ." And in Yugoslavia, it is clear from his remarks, certain methods of personal evangelism remain useful: the Gospel can be preached inside the churches and friends can be invited; Christians can witness in the homes of friends or "in friendly everyday conversation with someone who will listen to our experience with the Lord or who asks us about our hope. . . . We have freedom to converse after church services or evangelistic appeals in the church and can talk with children in the Sunday School. Another wonderful opportunity for personal evangelism is through records. Sometimes believers who lack courage to witness will invite friends to their homes to hear Gospel messages and songs on records." When one senses this desire on the part of believers in Eastern Europe to witness for Christ under highly adverse conditions, one cannot but be stirred to a sense of personal guilt over the constant neglect of wider opportunities in the Free World. Their obedient devotion to Christ, within the range of their limited opportunities, reflects a quality of dedication that shames us and spurs us to greater evangelistic zeal.

But that is not the only observation to be made on Dr. Horak's viewpoint. For his total disinterest in the question of the duty of government to preserve human rights (and the special importance of religious liberty in view of the apostolic insistence on freedom to fulfill the Great Commission) has serious implications. Dr. Horak asserts that "In today's world Christians in almost every country have more opportunity to witness than they had in Rome in apostolic times. . . . The first Christians . . . were unable to have many evangelistic crusades in that day, for enemies soon scattered them." Here any statistical comparison seems to be largely speculative, although Harold Kuhn of Asbury Theological Seminary also asked the World Congress to "recall that originally Christianity was projected into a world that was under a sophisticated totalitarian system" and that St. Paul and the other apostles "no doubt . . . felt frustrated and limited in many aspects of their work." But more is at stake than quantitative comparisons. Hudson Armerding, president of Wheaton College, has remarked pointedly that had the nineteenth century (which Kenneth Scott Latourette calls "The Great Century" in the missionary advance of the Church) been marked by "the militant opposition so characteristic of today's totalitarian regimes, the history of the expansion of Christianity might have been markedly different." One can, in fact, project this observation back upon the first century, and ask whether, had the apostles not chosen to make an issue of religious liberty, Christianity would have experienced a far different and discouraging outcome on the world scene.

It is interesting, therefore, to find an institution like Wheaton College today emphasizing the importance of a political career, and encouraging students to serve in government posts where universal justice—including the preservation of rights—ought to be a central concern. Dr. Horak says of Yugoslavian believers, "if it is impossible to fish for men's souls with large nets of mass evangelism, we still have the privilege of fishing patiently with a rod!" But if religious freedom is not a right, even fishing with a rod can be forbidden—and indeed has been in North Korea, and almost so in Red China. Fishing for men is more than a Christian privilege; it is a necessity for all who own Jesus Christ as Lord—and no man, and no government, has legitimate power to prevent man's obedience to the commands of God. That is why, alongside Dr. Horak's emphasis that "the most important thing for Christians today is not to simply talk about their opportunities, but to use them properly," we may well range a caution to the World Congress by a San Francisco Lutheran minister, Ross F. Hidy: "Evangelism is always in danger of being given a place out of proportion to the total concerns of Christian faith."

If one is tempted, however, to think that Dr. Horak's view reflects simply an accommodation of evangelical loyalties to political realities in the communist world (in line with the position of East Zone churchmen in the World Council of Churches, who likewise draw an extreme line between church and state—except with regard to socio-political positions in the Western world!), he must not quickly leap to that conclusion. For even in the Free world many Evangelicals stress the contrast between *church* and *world* so as to depict necessary Christian engagement only in terms of evangelism. Their lack of optimism over world history stems from an emphasis on the transcendent aspect of the Kingdom of God, viewed in relation to the Second Coming of Christ, as opposed to optimistic liberal theories that ignore not only the Lord's return but the importance of individual regeneration for reversing the decline of the historical process. The Christian hope of the Lord's return not only forms an essential part of the Gospel message alongside the cross and resurrection of Jesus Christ, but it stands, as Ernst Schrupp, director of the Wiedenest Bible School, stresses, in a direct relationship to the evangelistic task: before the Lord returns, the Gospel must be preached throughout the world (Matthew 24:14, cf., Romans 11:25). As Raghuel Chavan, moderator of the General Assembly of the Christian and Missionary Alliance of India, reminded the Berlin delegates: "Our Lord left a distinct programme for His Church to carry out in His absence, and is coming again when the task is completed." The Evangelical vision of the new society, or the Kingdom on earth, is therefore Messianic, and is tied to the expectation of the return of Jesus Christ in glory. It is distrustful of world power, of attempts to derive a just society from unregenerate human nature. And this verdict on human affairs is fully supportive of the Biblical verdict on fallen history. With good reason, therefore, W. Maxey Jarman, the distinguished Southern Baptist layman who is chairman of GENESCO, Inc., reminded the World Congress that whether the trusted means has been wealth, organization, military power, or political power, all have failed to change human nature and to achieve a new world, and that the mission of the Church is to spread the Word of God "so that more individuals will be brought to a saving knowledge of Jesus Christ and will have access to love that changes lives and accomplishes great deeds." Mr. Jarman's comment on political dynamisms is especially negative: "A careful study of history must convince us not only of the danger of political power with all of its corruption, but also of the futility of trying to change human nature through legislation or political influence. And it is only by changing human nature that we are going to make this world a better place. . . . It is evident that modern civilization and political power have been unable to achieve stability in the world, much less bring integrity and intelligence into the affairs of men. . . . The problems of racial integration demonstrate the inability of legislation, of military force, of money to produce the right kind of relationship. It is all too evident that if results are to be achieved, there must be some change in the hearts of people."

If now one correlates the emphases of Horak and Jarman, though they come from wholly divergent political theaters, one gets three theses that Evangelicals everywhere fully accept: (1) that whatever measure of freedom for the Gospel exists anywhere should be used maximally for the fulfillment of the Great Commission; (2) that the power to change human nature and to transform society lies wholly in the Gospel, and not in political or secular power; (3) that political power has shown itself historically to be mainly corrupt and hostile to the claims of God. But a fourth premise—that Christians therefore are diverting their energies from legitimate priorities when they seek to promote human rights in relation to government and law—is often sheltered by the third thesis, and Evangelical disagreement over its propriety points to one of the most important frontiers of contemporary discussion over social engagement.

Granted that only God on the basis of creation and redemption ultimately assures the dignity of man, is civil government as part of its divinely ordained mission to preserve the equality of all men before the law? And is this requirement of nondiscriminatory treatment something that may be left among Christian believers to love rather than law—or do even Christians, because of their partial rather than total sanctification, need to be confronted with the legal requirements of justice? Granted that only the regeneration of human nature changes the inner disposition and nature of man to do the right, does the fact that sanctification is a process, and that even twice-born men are not glorified in this life, and that Christians are often influenced by their environment and culture, argue that grace, which is the rule in neighbor relations, cannot wholly replace law in public relations?

William Pannell, a Negro evangelist and member of the executive staff of the Detroit Youth for Christ, told the World Congress that "ideally and scripturally" it is true that changing individuals is the only way to change society. "But this traditional view," he added, "is now being used as an excuse for almost complete non-involvement at all levels. . . . I am well aware of the pitfalls here and of the justifiable criticism aimed at those whose only gospel is social activism. But the other image of a conservatism that is pro-status quo is equally regrettable. It seems reasonable to expect that those who decry the methods employed by those seeking human rights would offer a suitable alternative. To declare that morality cannot be legislated is worse than spitting into the wind. Apparently it cannot be experienced in church either. . . ." Pannell spoke pointedly to surviving patterns of discrimination: "Something has happened to the dream of 'inalienable rights' . . . Something also has happened to that more fundamental vision about men being 'all one in Christ'."

As editor of *Christianity Today* I have long emphasized the need of the institutional Church to return to its evangelistic priorities and to the proclamation of the commandments of God. I do not think it is the prerogative of the Church as an official body to engage directly in politics—whether the endorsement of particular political parties, candidates, or legislation. Christians as individuals do indeed have the duty, to the limit of their competence and ability, of engaging directly in the determination of public issues as they seek in good conscience to particularize the principles of social righteousness in terms of various political options. The corporate Church, however, becomes spiritually vagrant if she becomes a political agency; her mission rather is to proclaim the revealed will of God, including the divine standards by which the world order will be judged, and which criteria Godly people ought therefore to promote and support in the public order.

In my opening remarks to the World Congress I emphasized that Evangelical Christians have a message doubly relevant to the present social crisis—in which the question of race bears so large a part, both inside and outside the churches. For they know *the God of justice and of justification*—and if they faithfully proclaim and practice the implications of this message they can point the way beyond the present stale-mate in the controversy over race. Evangelicals have been making large strides in the realm of inter-personal relations between races; the sharp repudiation of racism by the World Congress and its clarion call for inter-racial good will, on the basis of a common humanity grounded in the divine creation and unity of the race, should reinforce racial understanding and cooperation both in the churches and in the community. But it remains for Evangelicals to identify themselves conspicuously and publicly with Negroes and others in the struggle for equality before the law. It is not the task of the institutional Church

to promote legislation, but it is the duty of Christians to
advocate and support good laws and to lead the way in
obeying them. If only regeneration can change human
nature, Evangelical Christians now have a dramatic opportunity to show what new life in Christ achieves that
unregeneracy and mere humanism lack. It is this demonstration to the world, of Evangelical dynamisms, that supplies one of the greatest opportunities of Christian witness
in Evangelical circles today—and in a sense the social crisis
for Evangelical Christianity turns on whether or not we rise
to it. Whenever Christianity has been strong in the life of
a nation, it has had an interest in both law and Gospel,
in the state as well as the church, in jurisprudence and in
evangelism. The Christian believer knows that there is a
secret inner connection between the transcendent justice of
God and the secular law of the state, and that ideally they
will coincide. But the Church has the task of renewing men
spiritually and morally so that they will aspire to do the
good; the Church has no mandate to impose sectarian dis-
tinctives upon the world by legal compulsion. Revealed
moral principles, however, are universally valid; God's
commandments will supply the basis of the final judgment
of the human race. God makes equal demands upon all
men before His moral law; ideally the state, as a minister
of justice, is also to enforce statute law indiscriminately.
Those who know that God deals with men justly and not
arbitrarily, and who also have a share in the justification
that reinforces His justice in the grace of Golgotha, stand
today at the crossroads of crisis in modern civilization. If
they find vision for our day, they can put the world on
notice regarding God's claim in creation and redemption,
by calling men everywhere to behold anew the demand for
justice and the need for justification.

In thus confronting the social crisis, Evangelicals will
face the question of social structures not in neo-liberal di-

mensions, but in and through the larger issue of God's created orders of society. Marriage and the home, labor and economics, the state and culture are all in crisis today and to these realms the Bible has much to say without either losing the Church in evangelism only, or losing the Church in secular humanism. The current reduction of basic Christianity to *agape* defined in terms of social and political initiative for others ends up with a falsification of the Gospel. As Hans Rohrbach, president of Mainz University, puts it, "The correct Biblical statement 'God is love' (I John 4:8) is inverted into the incorrect humanist slogan 'love is God'." The recent formulas, in fact, tend to view *agape* as selfless human love, and an appeal to Jesus is retained for emphasis on His humanity as the supreme example of love and service for others. But, as a correspondent of the London *Times* points out, this tendency easily leads to an Arian-Humanistic denial of Christ because it passes over His divinity. *"Agape* is not just human love, however selfless, but a distinctive and unique love that flows from the Holy Spirit and is God's own love given in Christ to men" ("Reasons for Non-Success of the Non-Church," London *Times,* November 26, 1966). A program that emphasizes good works and neglects the great credal affirmations of Christianity has in fact little to distinguish itself from an adult version of the Boy Scouts.

If the essence of the new birth is personal engagement in the social struggle, one has difficulty not only in squaring this ideal with the teachings of Jesus and of Paul, but also in squaring it with its identification as a uniquely Christian experience. While the New Testament as well as the Old emphasizes the social responsibility of the believer, it views good works not as the substance of regeneration but as a consequence and evidence of it. A believer deprived of opportunities of social engagement does not on that account forfeit new life in Christ. While Christianity—and

particularly Evangelical religion—has carried a wide vision
of social idealism in espousing the possibilities of Christian
culture, a one-sidedly public, external definition of regenerate morality easily loses any essentially Christian orientation. Under its influence some professedly Christian fel-
lowships have already widened their identity to include a
variety of religious faiths and even unbelievers in order to
achieve flexibility for social involvement. But what then
becomes of the identification of *Christian* regeneration
with social engagement?

The neo-Protestant view, in fact, substitutes the notion
of corporate salvation for individual salvation. So Dr. E.
Edmund Perry, professor of history and religion at North-
western University, told the Methodist Council of Evangelism in November, 1965, that seeking to save an individual's soul is not evangelism and is no longer even
Christian. "I abhor the notion of individual salvation," he
asserted. "Christian is a societary term." (Report by Adon
Taft, religion editor, in *The Miami Herald*, November 17,
1965). Dr. Perry added that old-time evangelism services
are not as much evangelism as are civil rights marches. It
is clear that the concept of community or social action is
here proposed as a preferable alternative to individual or
personal experience of Jesus Christ as Saviour from sin.
The authentic mission of the Church is thus asserted to
be that of changing the structures of society and not that
of winning individual converts to Christ as the means of
renewing society. The "gospel" is said to be addressed not
to individuals but to the community.

This theory is connected with a further assumption,
that individuals as such are not lost in the traditional
sense, and that the mission of the Church in the world is
therefore no longer to be viewed as the regeneration of a
doomed world, but the Church is rather to use the secular
structures (political, economic, and cultural) as already

on the way to fulfillment of God's will in Christ. Direct ecclesiastical engagement in political campaigns, in civil rights demonstrations, endorsement of legislation, and advocacy of government welfare programs become preferred means of fulfilling the Church's mission in the world.

This universalistic view that the social order is to be considered as a direct anticipation of the Kingdom of God, whose cosmic rescue and redemption is held to embrace the totality of mankind, regards Christians as the vanguard of a New Society to be achieved through politico-economic dynamisms. Redemption is defined primarily in terms of dynamic change at the frontiers of social injustice. The new birth, suggested one philosophy professor on a church-related campus, consists in the active protesting of racial injustice. Regeneration is not viewed as a supernatural work of the Holy Spirit whereby, on the ground of Christ's redemptive work, one is restored to personal fellowship with God, receives a new charter freed of dominion by sin, and in love devotes himself obediently to God's scripturally revealed moral principles. It is humanistic devotion (especially political engagement) in behalf of one's fellow men. Those who see compulsory legislation as assuring a just society readily view eternity as a realm wherein divine constraint assures the redemption of all men.

The Evangelical reply to these positions does not dispute the fact of God's requirement of social justice and condemnation of social injustices, or that His redemptive purpose has sweeping cosmic implications, or that He deals with mankind on a racial as well as individual basis, or that regenerate Christians must give evidence of salvation by a life of good works. The Christian message intersects not only with the personal interest of the individual but with the public interest of society. The sensitivity of Christians is not to be sealed off from the complex structures of economic, political, and cultural life, but, to the extent of their ability and competence, the dynamic witness of believers is to carry over into the social arena.

What the Evangelical disputes is the activistic redefinition of evangelism in the direction of existential social engagement; the virtual replacement of interest in supernatural spiritual dynamisms by secular sociological dynamisms; the promotion of unscriptural universalistic premises; and the loss of Biblical orientation to the need of personal faith in the redemptive work of Christ as the sole means of deliverance from the wrath of God.

But Evangelicals dare not, on the account, withdraw from the world into a ghetto-Christianity by shunning the social implications of the Gospel. Their first duty to society consists, of course, in preaching the evangel. Bishop Chandu Ray of Pakistan insists that the greatest hindrance to the Gospel in the world of unregenerate men lies in their endeavor to prove their own righteousness, and their refusal to submit to God's righteousness. Not social activism, but the preaching of redemptive grace, will expose man's need of redemption. Yet it is also true, as Paul S. Rees says, that "if the Church today is to awake to the full authority and splendor of her mission, she must realize that her evangelism consists as truly of what she *is* as it does of what she *says*." W. Stanford Reid, head of the department of history in Wellington College, University of Guelph, Ontario, Canada, rightly emphasizes how unfortunate it is that some "who would evangelize the world today present unattractive and even repulsive lives which tend to contradict their message of the love and grace of God in Christ." It is remarkable how many churchmen today in posts of leadership minimize the importance of the Biblical virtues in the lives of believers, as if the doctrine of personal sanctification were somehow to be left to the "purity nuts," while they excuse transgression of God's commandments in the name of the new morality or telescope social ethics to the realm of political pressures. Some of these same leaders offer not a word of criticism against communist governments that wholly deny churches the right to social and political action.

Yet Harold Kuhn appropriately reminds us that not only the East, but the West also, has "failed to remember that God is creator of the material order" and that "covert materialism may offer an oblique form of opposition to Christian evangelism that has far more frustrating aspects than does creedal and dogmatic materialism." Not only must Evangelical Christians in affluent societies themselves learn much more about the stewardship of possessions as an entrustment to be used in relationship to others, but white missionaries abroad may also unjustifiably stimulate materialistic aspirations, as Howard Jones of Liberia points out. Recent ecumenical conferences that are concerned for modern man's material betterment more than his moral and spiritual betterment reinforce the notion that abundant life is to be found in the possession of things. One of the deepest issues faced by Evangelical Christians in their opposition to the Marxist attack on property rights is whether they can combine the defense of private property with an equally dedicated use of possessions as a divine stewardship. The estimated 40 million Protestants in the United States alone, by the contribution of a single additional dollar a year to evangelical causes, could make a remarkable impact in the fields of education, evangelism, and missions and relief efforts. In fact, $40,000,000 could not only establish an Institute for Advanced Christian Studies, but it could launch a Christian University. And in the current battle for the minds of men, evangelical Christianity needs the fullest possible enlistment of its intellectual resources.

The moment has come when evangelical Christians in the West ought not to waste their main energies deploring the lack of prophetic leadership by churches in the communist world; they should be taking the initiative to interpret the history of our times in relationship to the transcendent judgment of God and the opportunities for grace. Jean-Paul Benoit, president of the French Evangelical Alliance, finds a new opportunity for the Christian regeneration of man and renewal of society in the devastating collapse of recent secular alternatives. "If our century has been able to see, because of its very science and techniques, the drama of two world wars, gas chambers, and a recurrence of torture—is not, even because of this accelerated power, the greatest problem of the hour that of man, his conscience, his moral ideal and the strength which will allow him to live up to it? Others may advocate their ideals and their methods. We offer as our model Jesus, and as our victorious strength for regeneration His work accomplished for us, and offered to each of us." If evangelicals truly believe as they affirm, that justice and peace will increasingly prevail in history as men and nations seek and obey the will of God, no more relevant hour can be found than now to point to the Kingdom of God. It is obvious that human totalitarianism drifts invariably toward atheism and the demonic, however high its vocabulary about social justice and human dignity. And it should now be equally clear that self-government or majority rule is no guarantee, as Michael Cassidy of South Africa reminds us, of "good government and responsible rule." Hugh Thompson Kerr has somewhere said that "we are sent, not to preach sociology but salvation; not economics but evangelism; not reform but redemption; not culture but conversion; not progress but pardon; not the new social order but the new birth; not resuscitation but resurrection; not a new organization but a new creation; not democracy but the Gospel; not civilization but Christ. We are ambassadors, not diplomats." And in this characterization of the good news he is wholly right. But the will of God has implications also for sociology and economics and culture and social order. Man cannot live alone—he must live his life in society if he is to be truly man. Indeed, if he is to be ideally man—in the image of God—he must be told the criteria by which God will judge men and nations, that is, the standards by which the Creator expected human life to be ordered in obedience to His commands, and the message of redemption that regenerates men in holiness. In the crisis of our times the task and duty of evangelical Christians is to proclaim to men everywhere what the God of justice and of justification demands.

CHAPTER FIVE

Evangelicals and the Ecumenical Crisis

The current meaning of the term *ecumenism* has in it something of quite recent development. Initially the term indicated a gradual reversal of the process of denominational division and independency that had arisen from the sixteenth-century Protestant Reformation. Gaining momentum, ecumenism then signaled an effort to transcend the barrier between Protestantism and Eastern Orthodoxy. Now it seeks also to overcome the previous separation of Protestantism from the Roman Catholic Church and the much older division of Eastern Orthodoxy from Latin Christianity. In this complicated and unpredictable process, the nature of ecumenism itself underwent notable revision that had far-reaching consequences. The range of its redefinition may be measured by the fact that in its beginnings ecumenism was a cooperative movement of evangelical Protestant bodies that sought to advance evangelism and missions as their common cause. Modern ecumenism, in conspicuous contrast, lacks any driving commitment to evangelical theology and has, in fact, been wholly unable to reach an agreed definition of evangelism and mission.

Seen in an ecumenical context, the World Congress on Evangelism garnered a denominational participation that was in some ways more ecumenical than the dialogue within the World Council of Churches. Delegates to the Congress from 76 participating churches and groups were affiliated not only with mainstream ecumenical churches, but also with many churches that are not now inside that body and perhaps never will be. More significant, however, was the fact that conciliar ecumenism's long-standing neglect of evangelism as a primary concern was what had shaped the rising demand in the world Church for a global platform devoted to obedient fulfillment of the Great Commission. The proposal and projection of the 1966 Berlin Congress arose independently of the World Council of Churches, whose spectacular assemblies on church merger, faith and order, and church and society, had repeatedly neglected evangelism as a central concern.

W. A. Visser 't Hooft, for a quarter of a century general secretary of the World Council, long ago observed that the rise of modern ecumenism stemmed from a transdenominational concern for extending the Christian witness. The way was prepared, in Visser 't Hooft's words, "by co-operative undertakings in the field of foreign missions, home missions, and social service, by international youth movements—Y.M.C.A., Y.W.C.A., Student Christian Federation—by the Evangelical Alliance and national federations of churches. A new chapter began in 1910 when the World Missionary Conference met in Edinburgh under the chairmanship of John R. Mott" *(Twentieth Century Encyclopedia of Religious Knowledge,* Grand Rapids: Baker, 1955, "Ecumenical Movement"). In this early stage ecumenism was motivated by an unrestrainable ambition to evangelize the earth in a single generation—a longing which ecumenical Christianity has all but lost in the past half century.

It was significant that the Berlin Congress of 1966 registered growing impatience over any and all ecclesiastical forms that impede evangelism. Indignation was directed not only against non-evangelical structures, but also against evangelical fragmentation and competition that so often dilute evangelistic potential. An obvious concern also was the conciliar emphasis on merging churches while ignoring and displacing evangelism. Deplored, too, was the sentimental ecumenical disposition to regard all church members as Christian, whatever their spiritual regeneracy or unregeneracy, or their theological belief or unbelief. Yet perhaps an ecclesiastical institution that can embrace God-is-dead theologians, and hail Bultmann's demythology is in no position to distinguish believers from unbelievers in its own ranks.

Speaking against preoccupation with ecclesiastical forms at the expense of an authentic scriptural content, Walter Künneth, the German theologian, declared: "A church that bears a thankful sense of responsibility to its Reformation fathers will be concerned for maintaining the purity of the Gospel and its furtherance. It will therefore consider church forms, ceremonies, rites, and traditions of only relative value, and in no way necessary for salvation. The structure of the Church in itself is never 'sacred,' but, determined only on the basis of suitability, is oriented to implementing a purposeful proclamation of the Gospel. . . . The only valid consideration for the Church to realize at all times must be what serves the Gospel, its credibility, its deepening, its propagation." "What forms, customs, and ordinances must be removed, changed, or avoided," Künneth asked, "lest the Church itself be a burden to faith in the Gospel?"

As evangelicals see it, the irony of this current ecumenical predicament lies in the fact that the conciliar movement, passionately more concerned with changing social structures than with redeeming individuals, shows little disposition to expose its own ecclesiastical structures to judgment. Despite the fact that conciliar ecumenism professes to be unsure of its ecclesiological status, it continually acts in its dealings with others as if it were *the Church*. Those who remain outside its ranks, and who do not move at its formative frontiers, are made prime examples of ecclesiastical disunity and of disobedience to what the Spirit is supposedly saying to the churches. Although the conciliar process of mergers progressively substitutes larger denominations for smaller ones, somehow the mere fact of their conciliar affiliation is considered to protect them from the stigma of disunity.

Evangelical Christians, meanwhile, ask what requirement Christ's demand for obedient fulfillment of the Great Commission places upon every church, irrespective of conciliar affiliation or non-affiliation. They are not impressed by the enthusiasm for organizational unity shown both by the Second Vatican Council and by the World Council of Churches, while the Lord's evangelistic summons remains on the margin of concern. This attitude results not from the spirit of fundamentalist independency that pervades part of the evangelical camp. It grows, rather, from the conviction, after observing a quarter century of conciliar ecumenism, that mere "ecclesiastical joinery" that makes unity an end in itself soon raises as many problems as it solves.

In their missionary outlook evangelical Christians maintain the perspective not only of primitive Christianity but also of the modern ecumenical movement in its nineteenth century beginnings. A former president of Union Theological Seminary, Henry P. Van Dusen, has pointed

out that of 546 major events contributing to Christian
cooperation in the past 150 years, almost two in three
were connected with the cause of missions, and of these,
five in six occurred on the Church's missionary frontiers.
From the earliest instance of interdenominational association—that in London in 1819 of Baptist, Anglican,
Methodist, and interdenominational missionary societies
for "mutual counsel and fellowship"—the extension of
evangelical realities was a governing concern. Out of this
mutuality in mission sprang those great nineteenth century missionary conferences in Great Britain—at Liver-
pool in 1860, and at London in 1878 and 1888. These early
ecumenical efforts were evangelical to the core.

The Student Volunteer Movement for Foreign Missions
was founded in 1886 and in its first fifteen years almost
2,000 volunteers sailed to missionary outposts. Its watch-
word, "the evangelization of the world in this generation,"
according to John R. Mott, exerted a great unifying
influence by turning the thought of multitudes of Christians to the task of missions. By the time of its 1902
Toronto convention, the World Student Christian Federation embraced over 1,500 student organizations with
70,000 members; participants represented fifty divisions
and branches of the Church. Mott traced this unity to
the grip of Christian verities upon students who even at
the risk of death were willing to bear witness to Christ
to the ends of the earth. Hopefully, he said, the convention would restore confidence in the Church's missionary movement and would challenge a prevailing anti-
missionary spirit of criticism, unbelief, and indifference.

It would be difficult to state the Church's unifying
secret any more plainly than did Mott in a message on
"The Need of a Forward Evangelistic Movement." Here
are his words: "There is an element of immediacy about
the command of Jesus Christ that has never adequately

possessed a generation since the first generation of Christians. It is a simple proposition. The Christians now living must take Christ to the non-Christians now living, if they are ever to hear of Him. The Christians who are dead cannot do it; the Christians who are to come after us cannot do it. Obviously . . . each generation of Christians must evangelize its own generation of non-Christians, if Christ is to see the travail of His soul and be satisfied with reference to that particular generation" *(World-Wide Evangelization, The Urgent Business of the Church,* Chicago: Student Missionary Campaign Library, 1902, p. 150).

When one reads the annals of recent modern ecumenism, however, and views the World Council of Churches as the "copestone of the ecumenical arch" (the phrase is Dr. Van Dusen's), one quickly senses the striking change in this earlier ecumenical dream. No longer are evangelicial theology and mission the motivating and unifying center; the restless spirit of conciliar ecumenism is now far from evangelical.

So much has structural merger and organizational conformity become the dominating concern that when Dr. Van Dusen charts progress in Christian collaboration he classifies six major types in the following "ascending order of significance":

    i. *Consultation* for fellowship and mutual counsel.

    ii. *Comity,* i.e., agreement to divide responsibility and eschew overlapping or competition.

    iii. *Co-operation* in joint action.

    iv. *Federation* of churches or church agencies.

    v. *Union institutions.*

    vi. Full organic *church union,* in which the identity of the uniting bodies disappears or is wholly incorporated within the new church.

        (Van Dusen, *One Great Ground of Hope,* Philadelphia: The Westminster Press, 1961.

Whatever one may think of this index to ecumenical advance, it is obvious that the one undeniable development of recent modern ecumenism has been the erasure first of an evangelical image and then of a Protestant image. The ecumenical mood is still taking new turns, and no one can be sure of its ultimate disposition. But a movement that a century ago gained momentum as a trans-denominational evangelical witness, and early in this century acquired a pluralistic Protestant complexion, has since assumed a neo-Protestant character and now increasingly aspires to a post-Protestant-Orthodox-Roman Catholic identity.

Were this development to mark a revival of Biblical Christianity none would welcome the turn of events more than the evangelical Church. For it would then discover in ecumenism not only a deepening New Testament claim, but also a lively continuity with the beginning of modern ecumenical concern.

When the ecumenical spirit first awakened in the last century, it was essentially an effort of evangelical, inter-denominational cooperation for evangelistic and missionary objectives. Then liberal theology widely and swiftly changed the character of Protestant institutions, and the emergence of conciliar ecumenism—as in the Federal Council of Churches—coincided with the acquisition of a multiple theological image. With the subsequent formation of the World Council of Churches and its integration of Orthodox churches, conciliar ecumenism became neo-Protestant and its theological mixture blurred even more the distinction between scriptural verities and ecclesiastical tradition.

With the more recent Roman Catholic projection of Vatican Council II, the World Council of Churches could no longer preempt the term ecumenism. Neo-Protestant-Orthodox churchmen had no option but to recognize

Roman Catholic conciliar ecumenism as fully authentic as their own. As a result, contemporary Christianity now harbors two ecumenical frameworks of the conciliar type. Their representatives continually explore differences and agreements and probe effective interrelationships with each other, from time to time finding points of neo-Protestant-Orthodox-Catholic convergence or disengagement.

Fully as significant, though much less publicized, is the emergence of an evangelical ecumenical vanguard that is quite distinct from neo-Protestant-Orthodox-Catholic merger interests. Evangelical Christians consider the Roman Catholic variety of conciliar ecumenism an unpromising alternative, because of its hierarchical and sacerdotal commitment. And they are increasingly distressed over the course of the World Council of Churches. For more than a generation evangelical Christianity in Great Britain and America has reacted restlessly to the conciliar imposition of a liberal image on Protestantism. In the United States the atmosphere of protest soon nourished such movements as the National Association of Evangelicals and the American Council of Christian Churches, while in Europe the British Evangelical Alliance and the German Evangelical Alliance increased in vigor. The World Evangelical Fellowship marked the emergence of a skeletal international organization. These movements were not really *conciliar* (despite A.C.C.C. use of the term "council"), but nonetheless constituted a type of interdenominational ecumenism not unlike that in which the modern ecumenical movement had its first origins. A significant difference was that both N.A.E. and A.C.C.C. served mainly as a rallying point for evangelicals outside mainstream churches, although, N.A.E. refused (in contrast to Carl McIntire) to stigmatize all N.C.C.-affiliated churches as apostate. Another difference was that they institutionalized evangelical differences as a protest against the prior conciliar institutionalization of pluralistic perspectives.

Two important changes in the current religious situation are forcing the conciliar movement to recognize a rising evangelical tide, and to concede that evangelical momentum in contemporary Christianity runs deeper and wider than neo-Protestantism had been willing to acknowledge.

One change is an obvious transdenominational cooperative tendency in which evangelical ministers and laymen are being bound together in conspicuously larger relationships than those of the N.A.E. or A.C.C.C. Southern Baptists, Missouri Synod Lutherans, Nazarenes, and other groups have been reaching out toward larger liaison across denominational lines on a specifically evangelical base, particularly but not only in the realm of evangelism. Gathering on an informal basis, influential leaders are continually probing new areas of united witness and action with evangelical believers inside and outside the conciliar movement, and are thereby shaping a pattern which makes institutional ecumenism a matter of indifference in the achievement of their priorities. What specially disturbs many evangelical ministers and laymen in mainline denominations is the conciliar blunting of historic Christian theology, the utter breakdown of conciliar evangelism, and the frequently radical turn of contemporary ecumenical ethics. They seek, however, to move beyond polemics to the elaboration of an authentic evangelical alternative.

The second change is the growing interest of evangelicals within the conciliar movement itself in a type of evangelical ecumenism that diverges markedly from conciliar ecumenism. This development results from slow but painful disillusionment over the steady drift of the N.C.C. and W.C.C. toward unevangelical goals. For many years conservatives were told that the World Council was more evangelically oriented than the National Council, and

that American liberalism stood to the left of European in-
fluences. But recent trends have erased that appeal as
Continental theology declined to an existentialist plateau,
as the American liberal espousal of social revolution made
itself felt in the W.C.C., and as the confusion over definition of evangelism pervaded the entire conciliar movement. Moreover, the election of Eugene Carson Blake as
general secretary of the W.C.C. gave crowning evidence
that American and Continental ecumenism coincided in
their essential emphases. The enlistment of the institutional
Church as a direct political force, the eager promotion
of pluralistic theology in the seminaries, the revision of
confessional standards to advance church mergers, the
polite tolerance but skillful outmaneuvering of evangelical leaders, the readiness to impugn motives and to penal-
ize those who challenge or impede ecumenical ambitions
—such recent tendencies made evangelical churchmen
question the adequacy of conciliar ecumenism for achieving adequate Christian unity.

The mounting interest in evangelical ecumenism gains
new signifiance through the large numbers of interested
evangelicals in the old-line denominations. Many of these
mainstream evangelicals did not respond to previous interdenominational movements like the National Association
of Evangelicals, for example. But they have responded
to such cooperative projects as the Billy Graham evangelistic crusades. *Christianity Today* is now widely credited
as providing leaders of evangelical thought with an influential theological forum—a forum denied them by many
of the established denominational journals—to register
their opposition to the current deviations and to plead
for sound alternatives.

In a recent essay John A. Mackay, former president
of Princeton Theological Seminary, estimated that one-
fourth to one-third of the conciliar constituency in the

United States is theologically conservative. This figure is widely thought to understate the number of Protestants in the National Council who remain loyal to historic Christian beliefs. But even on the basis of this minimal estimate, by combining the ten million evangelical Protestants inside and 25 million outside the conciliar framework one arrives at a total of more than 35 million evangelicals in the United States alone. While the figure is probably too low—and 40 million may be taken as a sound estimate—it nonetheless dramatizes the fact that no segment of American Christianity has been as unrepresented by conciliar ecumenism as is this large evangelical constituency.

The World Congress on Evangelism gave solid evidence that evangelical ecumenism has already garnered world momentum at the evangelistic level. Despite secondary theological differences, this spontaneous movement shares a firm commitment to historic Christian doctrines that sets it apart from the theological plurality and vacillation of the World Council. In respect to affirmation of the ancient ecumenical creeds, the evangelical force has larger affinities to Roman Catholicism than to the neo-Protestant-Orthodox conciliar complex. Yet for evangelicals the issues raised by the Reformation remain to be debated—and, moreover, they are aware that some radical forms of modernism have also invaded Roman Catholicism.

As evangelical ecumenism gains visibility on a transdenominational world basis, conciliar ecumenism's recent repression of its evangelical component becomes the more apparent, and some conciliar spokesmen seek fuller reflection of evangelical views in the ecclesiastical dialogue. Conciliar leaders have more aggressively pursued conversations with evangelicals (particularly those still outside the conciliar complex), alongside their much more extensive and elaborate conversations with Roman Catholic participants. Their goal is to promote understanding and enlistment of larger evangelical participation in conciliar activities. But evangelicals outside the conciliar framework repeatedly emphasize that the N.C.C. and W.C.C. have routinely failed to reflect the convictions of their substantial number of evangelical affiliates, and have preferred to exalt almost every radical alternative not only to equal but to preferential representation in dialogue and platform participation. Not only is the evangelical voice given little program participation, but it has also had paltry representation on the W.C.C. Central Committee of 100. Only if much of the Orthodox representation is counted, and the term "evangelical" stretched far beyond its American understanding, can the Central Committee be said really to include a bloc of evangelicals. The fact is that no substantial body of belivers is as unrepresented in the conciliar power structure as the evangelicals.

A few W.C.C. spokesmen have conceded privately that it was "a shame" that the World Congress on Evangelism was not projected and sponsored by the W.C.C. which would, of course, have conducted it on a quite different base and with other participants. It is known that W.C.C. architect Visser 't Hooft—from the standpoint of universal conciliar ambitions—criticized the World Congress as an "evangelical parachuting of troops behind the lines." If one subscribes to Van Dusen's charting of ecumenical gains, the World Congress on Evangelism must inevitably appear as a retrogressive, primitive manifestation. Yet its significance as an evangelical manifestation of Christian unity lies in its return to the original transdenominational concern of the evangelical task force, prior to neo-Protestant pluralizing of message and mission that now characterizes the World Council of Churches.

It is noteworthy that the conciliar movement itself, after consummating a variety of church mergers with breathtaking speed, is now facing more serious obstacles to formal structural unity. The tensions between denominational confessionalism and unlimited conciliar union are increasingly apparent. Ecumenical spokesmen now muffle their bold earlier declarations that denominations are schismatic and wicked, and some even concede that full structural unity is a future eschatological expectation.

But what highly disturbs evangelical Christians is that conciliar leaders remain unaware that mutuality in doctrine and mission is the real key to Christian unity. In the absence of theological consensus and evangelistic commitment, ecumenical frontiersmen seem increasingly to concentrate on common social tasks and approved political goals as a hopeful bonding element.

Some hard-core organization men in conciliar ranks have long tried to stigmatize all evangelical dissent as fundamentalist radicalism. Yet despite the undeniable survival of pockets of negation and of independency of a fundamentalist sort, this maneuver has clearly failed because it does not fit the facts.

Evangelical ecumenism today is not simply a reactionary fundamentalism; its momentum is much broader in numbers and deeper in spirit than the independent Protestant groups that splintered from parent denominations in the liberal era. Nor is it only a matter of non-conciliar momentum like that supplied by the N.A.E. It reaches also to the so-called non-conciliar "third force" (Church of God, Nazarenes, Christian and Missionary Alliance, and so on); it is increasingly attracting the so-called "left wing" of the Reformation (Southern Baptists); and conservative denominations deriving from a Reformation tradition (Missouri Synod Lutheran). And in conciliar circles it reaches into almost all the mainstream churches —Presbyterian, Episcopal, Methodist, and others. In fact, some estimates place a larger number of evangelical

Christians within the conciliar movement than outside, despite the predominantly nonevangelical image maintained by its officialdom. Evangelical ecumenism today is therefore transdenominational, transnational, and even transecumenical, since it now often jumps the lines of affiliation or non-affiliation with any of the several current ecumenical options.

Although no formal organization shelters emerging evangelical ecumenism, it nonetheless has conscious identity. The Bible is its formal principle of authority; spiritual regeneration is its indispensable requirement for Christian life and progress; and the evangelization of mankind is its primary role for the Church. Pressures are mounting for a structural framework to coordinate evangelical effort for a dynamic witness to biblical realities. In an age in which denominations are losing their sovereignty, influential evangelical leaders are increasingly being asked why the sovereignty of Christ ought not to be reflected into the present scene by an ecclesiastical movement that gathers together the fragmented evangelical forces. But neither Billy Graham nor *Christianity Today* has thus far encouraged such a step, and during the World Congress on Evangelism it was explicitly stated to the press that the Congress avoided two perils — the further fragmentation of evangelical forces despite the wide variety of conservative participation in the Congress, and the premature coordination of forces into a global organization predicated on evangelical premises. Whether evangelical ecumenism will acquire structural and organizational forms now depends largely upon the extent to which conciliar ecumenism continues to repress, retard and reconstruct evangelical principles and priorities.

In Great Britain, where conciliar leaders are insistently advancing more church mergers despite substantial evangelical opposition, there is growing discussion of the desirability of a new Evangelical Church of England. Snide dismissals of Evangelist Billy Graham's ministry, as by the Archbishop of Canterbury, encourage many evangelicals to seek an ecclesiastical climate in which nonevangelicals cannot use their influence to impede evangelical effort. A study commission of the National Assembly of Evangelicals in Great Britain has stated that the time is not now ripe for evangelicals to form a United Church, but some impatient churchmen have urged Martyn Lloyd-Jones, minister of G. Campbell Morgan's Westminster Chapel, to lead such an effort. In October, 1966, Dr. Lloyd-Jones urged evangelicals to leave their denominations for the sake of a new church. "Everyone is talking Church unity except evangelicals. . . . The most pathetic thing of all is that our attitude to Church union is always a negative one. . . . Are evangelicals content to go on being nothing but an evangelical wing to the Church? Are they prepared to modify the existing situation, or to start afresh and go back to the New Testament?" Other churchmen, however, contended that the evangelical responsiveness of the Anglican Church should first be more thoroughly tested.

In the United States the continuing compromise of evangelical theology and evangelism, and preoccupation with social action, stimulates a creative interest in evangelical ecumenism that transcends both denominational and conciliar interests. The first significant sign of conciliar responsiveness to evangelical concerns came in December, 1966, at Miami Beach when the National Council of Churches scheduled Billy Graham to address a luncheon meeting during its General Assembly sessions. Graham has also been invited to address the fourth World Assembly of the World Council of Churches in Uppsala, Sweden, in 1968. Since the evangelist's supporters represent the largest bloc of evangelical critics of ecumenical perspectives both inside and outside the conciliar movement, some churchmen have urged his participation as a gesture toward conciliating the evangelicals. Conciliar circles reflect a growing interest in evangelistic themes: in 1966 an N.C.C.-oriented colloquium was held on the subject of conversion, a topic scheduled for further consideration in Uppsala; in June, 1967, the N.C.C. Division of Christian Unity will hold a colloquium at Notre Dame on evangelism in a pluralistic society; and an N.C.C.-W.C.C. study of congregational missionary structures is soon to be released.

Nonetheless the nature of conciliar commitment to evangelical evangelism remains very much in debate and the final determination of that commitment will be a major factor in deciding the direction of evangelical ecumenism. Bishop Otto Dibelius of Berlin told delegates to the World Congress on Evangelism that he had long ago urged the World Council of Churches, of which he was a former president, to anchor its spirit to evangelism, and to consider Graham its guiding star in an outreach to the masses. But the conciliar movement is still no nearer an agreed definition of evangelism than it ever was. That recognition was finally given to Graham's point of view on the conciliar platform must not obscure the fact that what he got was simply a hearing, not an official endorsement of his ministry. Spokesmen for the N.C.C. have long criticized traditional evangelism, and the Miami meeting of the General Assembly was no exception. The 64-page preassembly study book issued by Colin Williams, associate secretary of the Division of Christian Life and Mission, had a press run of 100,000 copies. Williams himself took the platform to stress that New Testament evangelism which emphasizes personal conversion is no longer adequate. In recent years the so-called "new evangelism," which stresses changing of social structures, has been invoked to justify the institutional Church's continuing intrusion into political affairs, repeated endorsement of legislative bills, espousal of specific positions on military, economic and social issues, and support of demonstrations to bring about political change.

In his remarks Graham swiftly destroyed the liberal myth that would identify evangelical Christianity with social indifference. A number of journalists and clerics quickly interpreted his combination of personal regeneration and social compassion as a conciliatory synthesis of ecumenical neo-evangelism and evangelical evangelism. Graham insisted, however, that true biblical social concern must be built upon authoritative proclamation and personal regeneration. Champions of the new evangelism considered Graham's participation at the Assembly a threat to their own position and, in a news conference that probed key differences that exist in the N.C.C. over evangelism, Williams emphasized: "There is a real clash, not just a fake war." Willis E. Elliott, of the United Church of Christ, told a section meeting that the World Congress on Evangelism was an affair of "verbalists" who were meeting "independently of existing ecumenical fellowship;" he dismissed its presentations as "piles of preachy scribal Bible expositions," and deplored some of the Bible messages as being just as dangerous as "the Red Chinese pollution." Elliott, an associate of the Division of Evangelism and Research for the United Church Board for Homeland Ministries, warned that N.C.C. differences with this evangelical position "may seem small but the chasm is wide." Then he hailed what he considered to be the chief ecumenical effect of the World Congress: to further dialogue between "Bible-defenders" and the rest of the Christian world.

The growing interest of conciliar ecumenism in evangelical evangelism is to be welcomed. The decisive question now, however, is whether the evangelical ingredient will be used for conciliar goals, or whether conciliar pluralism will be tested by evangelical realities. Now that the conciliar movement displays an enlarging interest in evangelical evangelism, evangelical Christians rightly expect a clear definition of the nature and content of evangelism, and of the course of action it implies. This is all the more proper since conciliar ecumenism is very specific in regard to legislative endorsements and to defining a course of social action which it relentlessly pursues to the distress of many evangelicals.

In the thinking of evangelical Christians, authentic evangelistic activity requires something quite distinct from programs frequently ventured under the banner of the "new evangelism." The issue between evangelical Christians and conciliar ecumenists is not that of evangelism versus social compassion. It lies rather in these considerations: (1) Evangelicals champion the authority of the Bible and are critical of pluralism in theology. (2) Evangelicals insist that authentic evangelism centers in the *evangel* (the good news of forgiveness of sins and personal regeneration on the ground of Christ's atoning death and bodily resurrection). (3) Evangelicals insist that *agape* deteriorates to mere humanitarianism if social action leaves out the evangel and promotes material rather than moral and spiritual betterment. (4) Evangelicals insist that social involvement is a Christian duty, but they repudiate the institutional Church's direct political pressures, endorsements of legislation, and advocacy of specific military positions; and they also repudiate ecumenical efforts to sell socialism as a Christian economic philosophy. (5) Evangelicals seek Christian unity but are lukewarm about promoting church mergers for the sake of organizational cohesion, rather than for the sake of theological unity and evangelistic momentum.

In invited remarks to the United States Conference for the World Council of Churches, held at Buck Hill Falls, Pennsylvania, in May, 1966, the author of this volume stated: "I make no pretense of speaking for the evangelical community as a body, nor for whole segments of it inside or outside the conciliar movement. But if I were interested in displaying ecumenical respect for conservative evangelicals, I would (1) make it a matter of conscience that one-fourth to one-third of the conciliar leaders are nominated by and from these evangelical Christians; (2) assign the leadership of the W.C.C. Committee on Evangelism and a majority of its membership to churchmen who support biblical evangelism, and not to those who repudiate it; (3) restore the Bible to proper centrality in the churches as the authoritative norm by which all pronouncements are to be tested; (4) encourage denominational publishing houses to seek out religious literature that advances biblical Christian faith instead of exploiting deviations; (5) seek proportionate representation for articulate evangelicals in the administration and faculty of all Protestant colleges; (6) call a moratorium on official ecclesiastical endorsements of political legislation until the churches agree on a proper role in public affairs, and refer legislators directly to their political constituencies for their views; (7) seek a renewal of moral conscience among the churchgoing multitudes by emphasizing divinely given principles of conduct and haunting the souls of men with an inescapable sense of public responsibility. These seven suggestions, if followed, would do more, I think, to build evangelical enthusiasm for ecumenism than anything else. If I were in the business of permanently merging churches, I would at least give this a try, although I must repeat that I am unskilled in this enterprise of restructuring churches and perhaps speak as a fool. I am confident, however, that such a program is likely to capture evangelical enthusiasm, and that it is to such compatible goals that evangelicals give themselves gladly.

"Many of us dare to hope that a new day is dawning. We do not brashly assume that the Kingdom of God produces only photocopies of ourselves, for it would then be a highly monotonous society. We long for a day when labels will fall away because believers so reflect the truth of God and show the love of God that the simple term 'Christian' recovers its apostolic purity. We weary of man-made mechanisms for repairing man-made deformities of the Church of Christ. We pray that the Lord of the Church may surprise us all, undeserving as we are, by a majestic renewal in thought and deed, before we are surprised, deserving as we are, by some unlooked-for visitation of judgment."

The challenge to evangelicals in these next years is not to allow arguments over structure and organization so to deplete their energies that they will themselves fail to do the things that, in the nature of the case, can only be accomplished by evangelicals because they remain a permanent evangelical duty. The production of virile theological literature in the Biblical mould, and the energetic fulfillment of the missionary task, and the deepest possible alliance of evangelicals across all institutional lines, are concerns that ought to remain in the forefront of vision. G. C. Berkouwer has said that from the conciliar movement conservative evangelicals can learn the urgent importance of the unity of the Church and the dangers of an unbiblical eschatology. John A. Mackay has said that from the conservative evangelicals the conciliar movement may learn the reality of Christian conversion, the importance of the Bible in the personal and corporate life of Christians, and the burden for world evangelistic mission *(Christianity Today,* May 27, 1966). The direction of ecumenism in the remainder of the twentieth century turns upon who learns what from whom.

Besides the ecumenical miscarriage of Christianity's evangelistic mission a second development increasingly governs evangelical attitudes toward the conciliar movement. That is the growing convergence between neo-Protestantism and Roman Catholicism. For the past decade conciliar leaders have aggressively pursued dialogue with Rome in the hope of including Roman Catholicism in the present Protestantism-Orthodox ecumenical combine. The Roman Catholic Church was invited into the World Council of Churches at its formation in 1948, but declined. Larger Roman Catholic participation in the World Council was seriously encouraged after Archbishop Ramsey's predecessor Geoffrey Fisher publicly promoted the idea of Rome's inclusion. Although Roman Catholic response was initially cautious, it is now becoming so vigorous that within another decade the conciliar movement may predictably undergo major changes that will reflect the greater Roman participation. Emphasis today falls on conciliar cooperation for common goals.

There is no visible prospect of world church union on the present conciliar basis; more likely is the emergence of some new structural manifestation, a troika presumably manifesting the major branches of Christendom.

One possibility is a commonwealth of churches compatible with Rome's claim to be the universal church. In this larger organization both neo-Protestantism and Roman Catholicism as now structured would go out of existence. Neo-Protestants would ignore the issues of the Reformation, but Rome would not necessarily disown the Council of Trent. The unifying emphasis would be the Bible *and* tradition. Rome would settle, some observers say, for a broadminded papacy: while the Pope would not exercise infallibility, at the same time he would not renounce the claim to infallibility. By conspicuous engagement in the world political scene the Pope would compensate for recent widespread losses of the Roman Church in the realm of theological and moral influence.

In major American cities Roman Catholics are already represented in perhaps two dozen local councils of churches, and the number of such councils grows monthly. Catholic spokesmen increasingly participate in N.C.C. conferences, and their growing role in N.C.C. commissions is now taken for granted. The N.C.C. staff already includes Roman Catholic personnel even in the Faith and Order Department. It is unlikely, however, that the Roman clergy would assume a voting role either on the N.C.C. Board or General Assembly, since this might seem to confer ecclesiastical dignity upon the present neo-Protestant-Orthodox ecumenical structures. Dr. John Coventry Smith, Presbyterian head of an N.C.C. committee that is probing relations with Catholics, thinks American Catholics will join "a National Council" in ten or fifteen years. The indefinite article is intended to stress the fact that any conciliar structure that includes 46 million Roman Catholics and 41.5 million N.C.C. affiliates will obviously reflect many differences.

It should not be thought that active participation of Roman Catholics in neo-Protestant conciliar programs would have only adverse consequences. Since the Roman Church is unlikely to regard dogma as officially negotiable, Rome presumably would push the World Council beyond its present skimpy theological basis in the direction of the great ecumenical creeds. Higher barriers to Unitarian participation would doubtless also be erected. Despite the World Council's present "trinitarian basis," Unitarians are associate members (though without voting rights on faith and order concerns) of the British Council of Churches, while in the United States they are in the local councils on a church basis rather than on a national organizational basis.

Nor are conservative Christians unaware of a genuine interest in evangelical realities by an increasing number of Roman Catholic laymen and some priests as well. There is no doubt that a vanguard of Catholics exists today for whom the new birth is a personal experience, who are trusting the atoning death of Christ for their salvation, who are discovering the Scriptures in a new and powerful way, and are witnessing to their friends about it. The opportunity of attending evangelical services, moreover, is shaping new attitudes of mutuality. One Roman Catholic layman recently remarked in an interdenominational gathering that whereas he had long been conditioned to associate Jesus Christ above all with the Virgin Mary and the Pope, his widening fellowship with Protestants had now encouraged him to connect Jesus Christ first of all with the Bible and the Holy Spirit. A multitude of Roman Catholic listeners have attended Graham evangelistic crusades with much spiritual profit, and not a few have made a personal commitment to Christ. Bold but timely was the invitation extended early in 1967 by Dr. Wayne Dehoney, former president of the Southern Baptist Convention, to Roman Catholics to take part in the mammoth evangelistic Crusade of the Americas to be sponsored by cooperating Baptist bodies in 1969.

It is clear that W.C.C-N.C.C. leaders today view Roman Catholics and Protestant evangelicals in two very different ways. Fragmentary efforts to overcome a long breakdown of dialogue with unaffiliated evangelicals are ventured in order to balance the public image; but evangelicals inside the movement are seldom dealt with as a distinctive body of opinion. Formative new opportunities are created for Roman Catholic spokesmen, but neo-Protestant pluralism continues to frustrate a cohesive evangelical witness within the conciliar movement. In recent years an effort to gain modest representation for conservative evangelicals in the Central Committee of the World Council proved abortive.

Enlarging participation by Roman Catholic churchmen in the conciliar movement deepens evangelical anxieties, both because of long-standing evangelical differences with Rome over theology and ecclesiology and because of neo-Protestantism's propensity for compromising evangelical doctrine and practice. Any convergence of neo-Protestantism and Roman Catholicism that dissolves the authority of the Bible and obscures first principles of the Protestant Reformation would place an intolerable burden upon evangelicals who now linger in the conciliar movement with waning hopes for an evangelical recovery from theological pluralism. Distressed as they are that the World Council as a movement cannot agree on what the Gospel is, and that individual ecumenists so diversely understand its essence, evangelicals are equally troubled by some affirmations of Vatican II and by modernist tendencies in the Roman Church.

Roman Catholic modernism has, in fact, drawn increasing fire from the Catholic hierarchy. To be sure, such criticism is as often directed against deviations from church tradition as against departures from Scripture—as when a Dutch priest recently reinterpreted the mass in terms of transignification (a new meaning) rather than of transubstantiation (a new substance). But Augustin Cardinal Bea's new book *The Study of the Synoptic Gospels* illustrates the rising indignation over the espousal of *Formgeschichte* and higher critical attacks on central Biblical miracles including dismissal of the Christmas story as a myth.

Vatican II seemed, moreover, to make peace with paganism, by an apparent implication that even atheists may be in the company of the saved, a position irreconcilable with passages like Hebrews 11:6, "without faith it is impossible to please God"; John 3:18, "He that believeth not is condemned already"; and I John 5:12, "He that hath not the Son of God hath not life." The Council's final reports speak of what was wrought in Christ "for the saving of the human race," and decl..re that "what He once accomplished for the salvation of all may in the course of time come to achieve its effect in all" (Walter M. Abbott, ed., *The Documents of Vatican II*, p. 587). Since neo-Protestant theology often has a universalistic bent, it is noteworthy that some Roman Catholic theologians now emphasize that the opportunity of salvation for all men may exist in ways we do not now understand. Some interpreters hail this trend as heralding a new era in the relation of Christianity to the non-Christian religions. In his book, *That the World May Believe*, Hans Kung writes: "It is . . . wrong to say: 'Only Christians can be saved. . . .' As against this, we Christians believe that *all* men, wherever and whenever they have lived, can be saved by the grace of God in Jesus Christ" (*That the World May Believe*, New York: Sheed and Ward, 1963, p. 113). Even Karl Barth, whose views look in the direction of universalism, has been prompted by theologizing of this kind to ask whether Rome might in time revert to a form of paganism where Christ is but a name.

What then does the future hold for evangelical Christians?

The number of conservative evangelicals in the United States is estimated at 40 million. Forty per cent of Protestants in the U.S. are not in the N.C.C. and as many as sixty per cent of the clergy and church members inside the N.C.C. are said to be evangelical. What force could bring together this great host that has no voice because it has no effective unity? Evangelical Christians have unlimited possibilities if they can escape either absorption or isolation.

They are not disturbed by a prospect of extensive changes in the present conciliar structures; as they see it, fundamental changes are desperately necessary. But a change in the mutual relations of the Christian churches ought to presuppose—as a guiding principle—knowledge of what a Christian church is. And since the conciliar movement seems unsure of its ecclesiological significance, it can hardly exhibit the ecclesiastical consciousness of a true church. For the majority of evangelicals a convergence of neo-Protestantism and Roman Catholicism in the present conciliar context is likely to cut short any further interest in the conciliar movement as a hopeful framework for evangelical Christianity. Such a convergence would imply not only a forfeiture of Reformation concerns, but also final and explicit abandonment of the Bible as the authoritative rule of Christian faith and practice.

Nor is there any future for the great bulk of evangelicals along the roadway of negation projected by Carl McIntire. Evangelicals need a positive program if they are to rally to apostolic priorities. Anyone who doubted that the American Council of Christian Churches is hostile to anything unidentified with its own institutions—evangelical no less than anti-evangelical—should have been convinced by the sad spectacle of McIntire's propagandistic distortion of the World Congress on Evangelism. This deliberate misrepresentation of the World Congress as leaning toward communism and toward conciliar ecumenism, and against Christian principles—a line of propaganda by which McIntire fueled the fears of his supporters—cancelled any remaining hope for constructively enlisting this movement for evangelical advance. The American Council professes to speak for many more members than McIntire has ever been able to confirm to the press, and A.C.C.C. leaders have learned to exploit the mass media far out of proportion to the movement's numbers. Among the American

Council's actual members, however, is a small band that not only resents the neo-Protestant take-over of American religious institutions, but also recognizes increasingly that the evangelical cause cannot advance simply by negation; they therefore do not share in McIntire's misrepresentation of such efforts as the Billy Graham crusades, *Christianity Today,* and the World Congress on Evangelism. They are acutely aware that McIntire's reactionary program has not nourished similar evangelical concerns on his own basis. But the American Council is too much a one-man program to allow such larger evangelical sympathies to gain momentum while McIntire survives as leader. Some spokesmen lament McIntire's miscarriage of this prospect.

But a great opportunity for evangelical transdenominational liaison nevertheless still exists, inasmuch as the World Council of Churches plays no important role in the life of most churches, except in that of a few younger churches who live by its economic aid. The conciliar movement cannot agree what Gospel truth binds Christians of all ages. Loyalty to the Lord of the Church impels evangelical Christians to seek the evangelization of the earth in our time; increasingly they ask what can be done to maximize the witness of believing Christians both to the unregenerate world and to a compromised and secularized Christendom. Knowing that the true Church is always susceptible to persecution by a false church, they recognize that their problem may soon be one not simply of repression but of oppression.

Are evangelicals merely to live by hope in these next years, trusting the Holy Spirit for new momentum, without making any effort whatever to unite for common objectives in an era of ecclesiastical turmoil? Are they to ignore the unexplored possibilities of evangelical fellowship and cooperation at the local level where the ecumenical movement is often little more than a clerical club for insiders?

In many parts of the land a conviction is growing that evangelicals—ministers and laity—should gather locally on the basis of the Bible as their authoritative rule of faith to ask what they can and ought to do together in these times of trial. Perhaps out of such gatherings an overwhelming spirit of repentance and renewal will come upon their ranks. Perhaps they will face the future with new confidence in the reigning and returning Lord. Perhaps a new sense of mutuality in mission will overpower them, so that they refuse to bequeath our generation to the cults, or to a conciliar superchurch. Perhaps, too, they will draw together in an external manifestation of their evangelical unity in Christ.

This year marks the twenty-fifth anniversary of the National Association of Evangelicals, which for a generation has institutionalized evangelical disappointment over the conciliar movement. To the credit of N.A.E., it has consciously sought to promote a positive cooperative program, and has kept open its doors to evangelicals irrespective of their ecumenical organizational alignments. But most evangelicals in mainline churches have been too preoccupied with denominational-conciliar tensions to engage in interdenominational evangelical programs except for evangelistic efforts. Even in this area N.A.E. participation was limited because of Christian Reformed conviction that evangelism is the responsibility of the church rather than of a cooperative evangelical movement. Meanwhile N.A.E. has acquired an image of being not only largely independent of mainstream churches, but also notably oriented to Pentecostal participation (about 35% of its membership is Pentecostal oriented).* Consequently it has gained little

*Carl McIntire's routine condemnation of Pentecostalists, and his periodic self-congratulation that they are not associated with A.C.C.C., must be correlated with a letter in which, in the early days of A.C.C.C. and N.A.E., McIntire urged the Assemblies of God to affiliate with the A.C.C.C. They chose rather to become identified with N.A.E.

enlistment from within such predominantly conservative bodies as the Southern Baptist Convention and the Lutheran Church-Missouri Synod, with both of whom N.C.C. has exploited relationships through its commissions.

The N.C.C.-W.C.C. is presently wasting its last opportunity to gain significant support for the conciliar program from evangelicals both inside and outside its framework. For one thing, in many cases it has responded defensively rather than enthusiastically to the evangelistic emphasis of the World Congress on Evangelism. While some significant impetus is being felt in this regard in several denominational programs, the top conciliar echelon continues to involve the institutional Church in political and economic debate as its primary task.

If the majority of evangelicals who are disillusioned by conciliar ecumenism are to find a congenial framework for cooperative endeavor, something will need to be done. Perhaps some new evangelical fellowship is due. Or perhaps N.A.E. must undergo a transformation and enlargement no less significant than the changes now so imminent in the neo-Protestant conciliar movement. Who knows but that the next decade will see the emergence of two world frameworks—a commonwealth of neo-Protestant, Orthodox, and Roman Catholic churches, and a global fellowship of evangelical churches.

Whether such an evangelical enterprise is new, or represents a significant revision of N.A.E., it will predictably inherit the A.C.C.C.'s hostility, as if it were simply the alter ego of the Catholic-Orthodox-neo-Protestant convergence. Whatever is unidentified with the American Council is almost invariably doomed to outer darkness by followers of the McIntire movement.

If a wholly new evangelical movement emerges, some tension between this movement and N.A.E. is inevitable, unless N.A.E. becomes an active affiliate from the first. If

N.A.E. maintains an unrelated existence, its constituency will become increasingly independent, increasingly pushed to self-promotion on an anti-conciliar rather than pro-ecumenical basis, increasingly critical of all mainstream churches, and increasingly dependent on extremist support.

Of the 40 million conservative Protestants in the United States, about twice as many are now inside the N.C.C. as are in either the N.A.E. or A.C.C.C., and probably more are in the N.C.C. than in both non-conciliar movements together. The national and world importance of such an evangelical fellowship might well rest upon the attitude of the Baptists. While the American Baptists and Southern Baptists have both retarded the effectiveness of a wide evangelical fellowship, they have done so for quite different reasons. Southern Baptists have traditionally remained aloof from all transdenominational efforts; their spokesmen are now increasingly enlisted on N.C.C. commissions, however. Northern Baptists were embroiled in the modernist-fundamentalist battle when N.A.E. was formed. When leaders of the Northern Baptist Convention pressed for denominational relations with N.C.C., Conservative Baptists withdrew from that convention to pursue their own program. Interest in N.A.E. lessened as a result. In the present ecumenical milieu, Baptists are caught between increasing pressures to enlist them either in the Baptist World Alliance or in the N.C.C.-W.C.C.; at stake is preservation of a Baptist witness, or merging that witness into inclusive ecumenism. Theologically, however, both movements now include all ranges of doctrinal deviation from advocates of the Living God to those of the death-of-God. For this reason more and more Southern Baptists are individually probing the possibilities of sharing in transdenominational evangelical fellowship. Southern Presbyterians also, disillusioned by the conciliar trend, show growing interest in such cooperative possibilities; it is widely thought that the Southern Presbyterian Church will refuse to join C.O.C.U., and that if it does, three-fourths of its members will supply the nucleus of a new Presbyterian denomination. It is noteworthy that, under the recent proposal for a Presbyterian Reformed Church in America, projected through a merger of Reformed Church in America and Presbyterian Church in the U.S., the amending procedure of the usual three-fourths vote of presbyteries required under current Presbyterian practice is lowered to a two-thirds vote—in apparent anticipation of the increasing resistance to intradenominational merger.

Reaction against the N.C.C. is often dismissed today simply as a matter of denominational hardening or different political emphases; dissenters now sense, however, that participation in a transdenominational movement that combines the evangelistic task with the fulfillment of social duty in an authentically biblical context would supply its own answer to distortions of motive. Similarly in Methodist, Lutheran and Episcopal churches one finds fresh probings for a possible new era of evangelical momentum. If a full-page call to transdenominational evangelical cooperation together with a clear statement of basis and goals were placed in local newspapers by interested church leaders, it would actively enlist multitudes of believers whose hearts are burdened over the sad plight of today's Protestant witness.

It is my personal conviction that the next ten years— the decade between now and the end of 1975—are critical ones for both conciliar ecumenism and evangelical Christianity. If conciliar ecumenism continues to repress the evangelical witness, and prevents it from coming to formative ecumenical influence, then conciliar ecumenism can only bog into a retarded form of Christianity. And if evangelical Christians do not join heart to heart, will to will, and mind to mind across their multitudinous fences, and do not deepen their loyalties to the Risen Lord of the Church, they may well become—by the year 2000—a wilderness cult in a secular society with no more public significance than the ancient Essenes in their Dead Sea caves. In either event the tragic suppression of the evangel would abandon modern civilization to a new Dark Ages. The New Testament Gospel would become merely another religious relic that men once held important, but that is now disclaimed by a calamitous age that has lost a sure Word of God.

APPENDIX

Facing a New Day In Evangelism

If we relate the Biblical revelation to the cavernous vacuums in modern life, the Creator-Redeemer God once again can fill our empty-souled generation as a powerful reality.

But Christ's disciples need not wait in hiding for a right moment to shock the world into its first glimmer of the supernatural, like a rodeo rider poised astride his steed for a sudden thrust down the chute to lasso an unsuspecting creature by total surprise.

We are not God's shock troops, serving as the first line of attack in this battle for the minds and souls of fallen men. The Lord Himself "rideth on a swift cloud" as Isaiah (19:1) declares, and the God of heaven and earth is no mere phantom in the sky. He emblazons His presence upon the whole creation. In the words of an Old Testament Psalm: "The heavens declare the glory of God; and the firmament showeth His handiwork" (19:1); in the words of a New Testament epistle, "Ever since the creation of

†Excerpted from my opening remarks as chairman of the World Congress on Evangelism.

the world His invisible nature, namely, His eternal power
and deity, has been clearly perceived in the things that
have been made. So they are without excuse . . ." (Rom.
1:20, R.S.V.). And John's Prologue tells us that the true
Light, the Logos, "lights every man" (1:9), that this Light
"shines on in the dark, and the darkness has never
quenched it" (1:5, NEB). Man the sinner does not walk
in total ignorance of the Living God; what marks him as
a sinner is *revolt against light,* both in Adam and on his
own account. Deform God's truth as he may, he is wholly
unable to extinguish the light of divine revelation that
illumines nature and history and conscience.

Despite man's universal spiritual revolt, the Living God
daily confronts the more than two billion persons of our
generation as a fundamental fact of their human existence.

The Cosmic Christ goes before us, convincing a rebel
creation that bears His marred image. The Great Apologist
inscribes the case for theism ineradicably upon the souls
of men. The Great Creator is astride His universe; daily
He confronts and corrals every last man and woman with
inescapable reminders of His power and deity and of the
judgment to come.

It need surprise no one that in communist lands older
people believe in God . . . nor that the very young everywhere do, for no one is born an atheist. Much of the
university world today no longer presents the case for
Christianity on its merits; communist campuses caricature
the Living God, while many Free World institutions simply
ignore Him. For this superficial disengagement from the
supernatural world our civilization already pays a terrible
price both in modern thought and life. Another generation,
its best minds aware of the reality and truth of redemptive
religion, will rise up to judge our superficial age. That
brighter generation may even now be living in its teens,

waiting for the army of God to sound the trumpet of faith.

Not only does the Cosmic Christ still confront man daily, but shattered remnants of the divine image in man still impel him daily to reach for a recognition that the naturalistic and atheistic theories now so current cannot really nourish.

Clamor for human rights is a hallmark of our times. But atheistic naturalism cannot sustain the case for enduring and universal rights. Communist theory suspends all human rights on the sanction of the totalitarian state, thus substituting the absolute state for the sovereign God. But only the divine image as a creation legacy and redemption latency supplies an adequate support for human dignity, endowing man with universal rights and duties, and reinforcing those rights even against the totalitarian state.

Not only does the Cosmic Christ go before us as the Great Apologist in our mission to mankind, but now as the Great Evangelist also convicts the human race in advance of our witness to the world. The eternal Word became flesh, the Logos sacrificially stepped into world history at the Father's bidding. The rejected Redeemer has sent the Holy Spirit to reprove the world of sin, of righteousness refused, of judgment inescapable. Now He bids us, as His co-workers, to take worldwide the good news of redemption in His Name: "As the Father has sent me, so send I you" (John 20:21). Thus He announces our integration with Him into the redemptive covenant of the Godhead, assigning us as ambassadors of reconciliation to stand between a perishing race and the Living God.

So extraordinary is the "good news" of Christ's Gospel that it can renew some of the lost dignity even of the unbeliever despite his atheistic distortion of spiritual concerns. What else reinforces man's sense of personal significance as insistently as his need to prepare for an individual destiny in eternity? Time and again, the evangelical reminder that Christ died for *my* sins and that eternal separation from Christ is *my* prospect unless the new birth is my portion, stabs awake the individual conscience so dulled by the secular forces of modern life.

If the machine age theatened to reduce man to a mere impersonal function, the computer age now threatens to dispense with him entirely. More and more the technological revolution seems to imply the insignificance and obsolescence of the individual. Social and political forces of our time likewise threaten the importance of the individual; Nazis elevated only the Nordic race to importance; communists sacrifice the individual to the collectivity; Western materialists reduce man to a machine for multiplying mammon. Modern philosophy and scientific theory both tend to demean the individual. In its search for laboratory explanations the scientific approach to life overlooks individuality in order to emphasize the universal and predictable, and thus minimizes the significance of human decision. Our recent focus on the sub-human world and on outer space makes man seem but one of a trillion specks of animated matter in the vast times and distances of the cosmos.

But the Gospel reminds all men of an inescapable personal destiny in eternity, based on a conclusive decision in time. Jesus was always reclaiming men and women whose sense of personal worth and identity had almost vanished. His redemptive power is still potent in a generation no longer quite sure of human dignity. By its urgent call to individual regeneration the religion of the Bible stands between the modern man and the daily erasure of his personal meaning and worth. It reminds every bearer of the debased image of God that he must some day stand before Him in whose image all godly men are even now being renewed.

But the Gospel of Jesus Christ does not remind men in a congratulatory way of their personal dignity and worth;

it upholds the dignity of man by offering a recovery of his squandered destiny through the forgiveness of sins and a new life. The God of the Bible is the God of justice and of justification. The Christian evangelist has a message doubly relevant to the modern scene: he knows that *justice* is due to all because a just God created mankind in His holy image, and he knows that all men need *justification* because the Holy Creator sees us as rebellious sinners. The Gospel is good news not simply because it reinforces modern man's lost sense of personal worth, and confirms the demand for universal justice on the basis of creation, but, also, because it offers rebellious men as doomed sinners that justification and redemption without which no man can see God and live.

The fact that the Christian messages speaks to the fragmentation of the self and to the derangement of society has also given rise to speculative religious theories that seek to restore the human personality or to promote social utopias, while they ignore the utter indispensability of the new birth for man's salvation. For several generations influential modern churchmen have ventured in Christ's name to reconstruct and revolutionize man and society while they discount the New Testament concepts of conversion and regeneration and reject the miraculous elements of the Bible, including our Lord's substitutionary atonement and bodily resurrection. Perhaps nothing attests the deepening apostasy of the professing Church as obviously as the ready secularization of the content of the evangel and of the mission of the Church.

For good reason we repudiate the inversion of the New Testament by current emphases on the revolutionizing of social structures rather than on the regeneration of individuals; we deplore the emphasis on material more than on moral and spiritual betterment; and we renounce speculation about universal salvation that cancels new life in

Christ as the precondition of present blessing and eternal bliss. What the Bible teaches, and what therefore we believe, still has more force than these popular ecclesiastical misconceptions.

But in these next days we must not simply deplore the evangelistic paralysis of the ecumenical movement; what the Church desperately needs is aggressive devotion to the right option. In the decade ahead we intend to proclaim the truth of revelation in full confidence of God's redemptive rescue of multitudes from many nations.

The early Christians knew themselves to be a new race —a race renewed, liberated from a doomed humanity and called to rescue others. Is it any wonder that men who have never been born again seek to remake man and society simply by reshuffling unregenerate human nature? Can we expect the unborn to depict a birth which they have never experienced? Recently a leader in a fast-growing denomination in the United States said: "Men need not live their lives away from God. Men need not live their lives burdened down with guilt. Men need not live their lives in wandering and aimlessness. God stands ready to receive us. . . . There is forgiveness and new life in Him" (Dr. Arthur B. Rutledge, in remarks to the annual Southern Baptist Home Mission Board conference in Ridgecrest, North Carolina, August 26, 1966). This emphasis by twice-born men on the Gospel invitation to the forgiveness of sins and the new birth can stir multitudes to seek and find redemption in Christ Jesus.

Lack of vital faith in the supernatural Creator and Redeemer sooner or later means the terrible loss of human dignity, social justice, and personal salvation. Outside of a rediscovery of the Gospel of grace there now remains no long-range prospect for the survival of modern civilization, but only a guarantee of its utter collapse.

Is it too much for men devoted to Jesus Christ to pledge

their hearts and lives to a bold new effort to give every man on earth in our time the opportunity to accept or reject the Redeemer? In the providence of God the staggering population increase coincides with the age of space travel and mass communication techniques. Do we have eyes to see new possibilities of evangelistic planning and witness? In the providence of God evangelicals of all lands and races are being drawn together across the ecclesiastical division of the recent past. Dare we look for interracial teams of evangelists who will circuit the earth in courageous confrontation of whole communities and nations torn apart by racial strife? In the providence of God the liberal and neo-orthodox revisions of Biblical Christianity are now sunk in a sea of anti-intellectualism, and modern theology wallows in the mires of confusion. Are we ready to call the student world to an earnest searching of those rational evidences for theism of which their intellectual peers for a generation have deprived them, and as skillful theologian-evangelists face these audiences with the full claim of the Gospel? Is it too much to ask God to make this World Congress an occasion for so melting and moving our hearts that each of us gains a deepened passion for winning souls that launches the cause of Christ upon a new tomorrow?

Let it be said of us that when we gathered here the man-made walls seemed formidable indeed, but only until the Risen One walked in our midst to remind us that He was crucified outside a sacred wall, and that He sundered even the seal of the walled-in tomb in which men laid Him, though it was the seal of the mightiest empire of His day. May it be said of us that we learned for ourselves in Berlin that to Him who appeared to walled-in disciples fearful of their contemporaries, even huddled behind closed doors, man-made walls pose no impenetrable barrier. Even as He showed the early Christians His hands and feet, and lent them new feet to carry the Gospel to Rome and beyond, new hands to minister to pagans forsaken by their own kin, new life in Christ that embarrassed the vocabulary of their day by its lack of adequate descriptives—so let us know the presence of the Risen One who speaks His commission anew to each of us and breathes upon us the Holy Ghost.

The early Christians knew that walls solve none of man's dilemmas, but only witness to man's diseases and his need for God's salvation. They rejoiced in a Redeemer who so renewed human beings into a single new humanity that men forgot whether they were Greek or Jew, circumcised or uncircumcised, slave or free; Christ became to them "all, and in all" (Col. 3:11). Their mandate was the Risen Redeemer's commission, and the only reason the ancient world rose from and above its pagan mires lay in man's response to the Gospel they proclaimed. Now, almost twenty centuries later, when much of the modern world is again pagan, that same concern brings us together. That same Gospel offers to persons of all races and classes and nations a fresh prospect of dignity and direction, of hope and happiness, of purity and power.

At the outset I said that without the full cooperation of evangelical Christians around the world—of whatever color, country, denomination or ecumenical identification or non-identification—we shall do little. Let me note in closing, however, that without the *Great Commissioner* we can do nothing at all. If we take the Great Commission seriously, we must take the Great Commissioner just as seriously: "He that believeth on me, the works that I do shall he do also. . . . Abide in me, and I in you. As the branch cannot bear fruit of itself, except it abide in the vine, no more can ye, except ye abide in me. . . . Without me ye can do nothing" (John 14:12, 15:4-5).

It is tragic when men who profess to serve Christ, in effect forsake the duty of evangelism; it is equally tragic when disciples who proclaim a devotion to the Great Commission try to "go it alone." When even theologians herald the "death of God," it becomes our double duty to manifest in our obedience the presence of the Living One.

Can we find for ourselves in these days what at first must have seemed almost incredible even to the early Christians, namely, that because Christ indwelt and transformed them, those who touched their lives acknowledged them to be a new race of men?

Will it be said of us: They came to Berlin pondering their individual tasks in a world out of joint; they returned like a host from heaven, unable to stifle their praise of Christ, their thousand tongues swelling into a single mighty voice, and their lives glowing with the radiance of messengers from another world?